William B. Kays
CONSTRUCTION OF LININGS ___ RESERVOIRS, TANKS,
AND POLLUTION CONTROL FACILITIES

John E. Traister
CONSTRUCTION ELECTRICAL CONTRACTING

William R. Park
CONSTRUCTION BIDDING FOR PROFIT

J. Stewart Stein
CONSTRUCTION GLOSSARY: AN ENCYCLOPEDIC
REFERENCE AND MANUAL

James E. Clyde
CONSTRUCTION INSPECTION: A FIELD GUIDE
TO PRACTICE

Harold J. Rosen and Philip M. Bennett
CONSTRUCTION MATERIALS EVALUATION AND
SELECTION: A SYSTEMATIC APPROACH

C. R. Tumblin
CONSTRUCTION COST ESTIMATES

Harvey V. Debo and Leo Diamant
CONSTRUCTION SUPERINTENDENT'S JOB GUIDE

Oktay Ural, Editor
CONSTRUCTION OF LOWER-COST HOUSING

CONSTRUCTION SUPERINTENDENT'S JOB GUIDE

Responsibility for construction in heavily populated and traveled areas belongs to the construction superintendent. (Pennsylvania Station, New York.

CONSTRUCTION SUPERINTENDENT'S JOB GUIDE

HARVEY V. DEBO B.C.E., P.E.
Construction Project Manager

LEO DIAMANT B.C.E.
Construction Engineer

A Wiley-Interscience Publication

JOHN WILEY & SONS
New York • Chichester • Brisbane • Toronto • Singapore

Library of Congress Cataloging in Publication Data:

Debo, Harvey V
  Construction superintendent's job guide.

  (Wiley series of practical construction guides)
  "A Wiley-Interscience publication."
  Includes index.
  1. Building—Superintendence. I. Diamant,
Leo, 1920-   joint author. II. Title.

TH438.D44   690   79-17979
ISBN 0-471-20457-9

Printed in the United States of America

10 9 8 7 6 5 4 3

Series Preface

The Wiley Series of Practical Construction Guides provides the working constructor with up-to-date information that can help to increase the job profit margin. These guidebooks, which are scaled mainly for practice, but include the necessary theory and design, should aid a construction contractor in approaching work problems with more knowledgeable confidence. The guides should be useful also to engineers, architects, planners, specification writers, project managers, superintendents, materials and equipment manufacturers and, the source of all these callings, instructors and their students.

Construction in the United States alone will reach $250 billion a year in the early 1980s. In all nations, the business of building will continue to grow at a phenomenal rate, because the population proliferation demands new living, working, and recreational facilities. This construction will have to be more substantial, thus demanding a more professional performance from the contractor. Before science and technology had seriously affected the ideas, job plans, financing, and erection of structures, most contractors developed their know-how by field trial-and-error. Wheels, small and large, were constantly being reinvented in all sectors, because there was no interchange of knowledge. The current complexity of construction, even in more rural areas, has revealed a clear need for more proficient, professional methods and tools in both practice and learning.

Because construction is highly competitive, some practical technology is necessarily proprietary. But most practical day-to-day problems are common to the whole construction industry. These are the subjects for the Wiley Practical Construction Guides.

M. D. MORRIS, P.E.

v

Foreword

Coauthors Harvey Debo and Leo Diamant never met or communicated. Though welded into this joint venture, they worked in tandem. Their only common bond was good construction.

Harvey V. Debo was a construction superintendent and project manager for over 40 years. Except for a couple of years on his own, he spent his entire career with Turner Construction Company, one of the world's larger, substantial firms. Leo Diamant worked for and with many small and large firms. For over 35 years he has been in all corners of construction contracting from inspection, lines and grades, design, estimating, troubleshooting, on through field work, supervision, and management. Debo was in charge of every size of building for Turner from a small pumphouse to New York's Penn Station–Madison Square Garden complex. Diamant won several Citations for his "crash" work at Cape Canaveral's launch facility. Both are aware, able men.

With Debo a quality job came before personality conflicts; he had to "make sure." Over all four decades Debo kept a notebook. "You learn something new on a job; you ought to be able to use it again some other time," he said; "Nothing useful should get lost down the cracks." I first met him when, as a "smart kid from college," I came on his job to be instrument man in lines and grades. That was the Summer of '42 when Turner was in a joint effort to build Griffiss Air Force Base at Rome, New York. A powerful, persuasive person, Harvey's positive personality soon converted my initial terror of him to complete respect both for the man and for his methods. He was a natural construction teacher who never let his BCE from Rensselaer Polytechnic Institute hobble his sense of pragmatism. This experience is now available for all. Harvey Debo died shortly after he retired. The Penn Station job was his valedictory. A triumph of the bare-handed man in the automated age.

But his notebook remains. Perhaps some of his practical ideas may "fly in the face" of some of today's systematized methods, but now and tomorrow there still will be problems that computers, models, and CPM won't solve. Only human beings must. They'll need some guidelines. Before he died Harvey organized his notes into a rough holograph script of 600 pages, in chronological order of job progress. He never refined or re-ordered them.

My Cornell classmate Leo Diamant did that for us. Diamant reworked Debo's basic material into current construction terms; reorganized it from time arrangement to follow the Construction Specifications Institute standard 15 division order, and finished the job.

Profuse thanks go to: John Saunders, P.E., President, Slattery Construction Co., New York; Lonnie Sciambi, V.P., McCloskey & Co., Builders, of Philadelphia; S. Peter Volpe, President, The Volpe Construction Co., Malden, Mass. (himself an author in this series); and Malcolm McLarren, P.E., Construction Consultant, Annapolis, Md., for their critical assistance and review.

This guide, the language, the ideas, are what Debo and Diamant set down over their combined 75 years of real building experience. They all have value, both on-the-job and historic. What these two superintendents forgot about construction could fill a book. But what they remembered did— this one! Use it profitably.

M. D. MORRIS, P.E.
Editor

Westbury, New York
September 1979

Preface

The construction superintendent is the final professional link in the chain of events that brings a construction project from its conceptional dream to its useful reality. It is the superintendent's responsibility to turn the architect's and engineer's drawings into the structure that all before him visualized. He must protect his employer's, the contractor's, interests, satisfy the demands of the architect, engineer and owner, and supervise with understanding and fairness all the many subcontractors on the project. He is expected to know everything when there seems to be no answer to a problem, and know nothing when others think they have a better idea.

The intent of this book is to provide the beginning superintendent, employed by the general contractor, with an awareness of the preparations required as each new trade commences work. It also will give the student in construction insight into the complexities of the field.

Rather than orchestrating solutions to problems, in most instances this book aims to call to the superintendent's attention situations that could cause problems. Every construction project has its own individual characteristics. Each problem may have several solutions. The superintendent, BY KNOWING HIS JOB WELL, will be able to come up with the right answers.

Figures 5, 7–9, 11–14, 18–38, 41, and 45–51 are reproduced by courtesy of Turner Construction Company.

LEO DIAMANT

Rosedale, New York
September 1979

Contents

1   General Conditions   1

2   Excavation, Pile Foundations, and Dewatering   20

3   Concrete   29

4   Masonry   100

5   Structural Steel and Miscellaneous Metal   108

6   Carpentry and Millwork   114

7   Roofing, Sheetmetal, Insulation, Sealants, Spandrel Flashing, Waterproofing, and Dampproofing   118

8   Hollow Metal, Hardware, Windows, Aluminum and Stainless Steel Entrances, Curtain Walls, and Glass and Glazing   122

9   Finishing Trades   125

10   Miscellaneous Specialties   133

11   Equipment   135

12   Furnishings   138

13   Special Construction   140

14   Conveying Equipment   142

15   Plumbing, Heating, Ventilation, and Air Conditioning   144

16   Electrical   148

17   Epilogue   150

APPENDIX   Industry Standards   153

Index   159

CONSTRUCTION SUPERINTENDENT'S JOB GUIDE

1

General Conditions

A construction project should be completed in the shortest possible time, at minimum cost, but not at a sacrifice of quality. This presents a great challenge to building constructors. It takes a lot of effort to meet this challenge.

Construction is one of the most fascinating occupations. Something is being accomplished that will stand as a monument for years to come, and anyone who has worked on the construction of a structure should take great pride in his accomplishments. This is why every construction worker (including the job staff) should make every effort to make the structure that is being built as nearly perfect a creation as possible.

This guide is written with the hope that the job superintendent, as well as all his assistants, will find in it some help to make the job a more efficiently run project.

Every job superintendent or project manager has a different idea of how his job should be run. Yet there are some basic steps that should be followed to ensure efficient, economical, and safe operation. We review these basic steps in this book.

Our description applies to an average building project costing up to a million dollars. The general contractor is assumed to be an average sized construction company that maintains a fairly small force in the main office. To back up the field force, an office force might consist of an executive who is the contact man with the owner and makes the decisions on a high level, a general superintendent who follows the job progress very closely, an estimator who when not estimating may fill in as a project manager or purchasing agent, and an accounting department; the jobs of project manager and purchasing agent, which consist of letting all subcon-

1

tracts and purchasing the main material items, must also be performed.

The field force on the job consists of a job superintendent (our focus) and assistant superintendents who handle various phases of the job.

These basic principles of building construction can also be applied to heavy construction work and all other types of construction work, including dam construction, road building, and installation of waterworks and sewer and water systems. Organizationally these jobs differ in certain specific detailed ways, but the running of the jobs is basically the same as in building construction.

1. Documents Required by Job Superintendent

Before starting any construction job, under ideal conditions, the job superintendent must have in the job site safe copies, not originals, of the following documents:

Copy of the contract with owner, for mediating small disputes. Know what to live up to.

Set of plans and specifications. Obviously *the* job guide. No deviations.

Copy of estimate. To stay on top of cost control and prevent runaway costs.

Copy of labor commitments. Labor is changeable as the weather. New men must keep old agreements.

Progress schedule. CPM or PERT Programmers must stick to it or explain.*

Copies of subcontracts. To keep subcontractors in line and performing; also helps purchasing.

Permits for use of sidewalks, streets, and so on. To avoid hassles with local police.

Of course no job starts under ideal conditions, and the documents follow as they become available.

At the beginning of the job, it is important to follow through with the paper work. The superintendent should be aware of the status of all subcontract negotiations. Permits should be actively pursued if all are not on hand at the startup of the job.

---

* The critical path method (CPM) and program evaluation and review technique (PERT) are two modern aids in scheduling complicated projects.

In addition to the documents above, one of the most important sets of documents consists of the shop drawings prepared and supplied by the subcontractors. We discuss the shop drawings in more detail as we develop the general conditions of the job and each trade's requirements.

2. *Visiting the Job Site*

As soon as a construction superintendent or a project manager is assigned to a job, he must visit the site to plan his office and plant layout. He must note with the engineers the proximity of other structures, in case underpinning is required. He should plan the positioning of his office and the subcontractors' shanties or trailers, as well as the form yard, the reinforcing rod yard, a place or storage pile for topsoil, backfill, and so on, the spotting of towers and concrete and mortar mixing plants, the location of ramps for excavating trucks, and electrical sources, sewers, and storm drains.

Other volumes in this series deal with ground water, soils, rock, equipment, management, steel, concrete, and other specific problems. The theme of this book is to allow a superintendent to walk onto a job site with plans under arm, and enable him, in his mind's eye, to envision the job as a going concern, then to help him get it there.

Starting the job requires the superintendent to make many decisions that he must live with throughout the project. A thorough knowledge of the plans and specifications is the superintendent's first priority. Setting up the project fence, the entrances, and the location of ramps for excavation is the next step.

If the work is in a city, the municipal traffic department should be contacted to provide "No Parking" signs where required. Street permits for containers and storage of material, if permitted and needed, should be obtained. This can be accomplished with the cooperation of the home office, once they know your requirements. Figure 1 illustrates the possibilities for problems to arise at a crowded urban site.

Since most jobs involve many subcontractors, it is important that you become aware of the trades that will be done with your own forces. Today a general contractor for building construction does a minimum with his own forces.

Fig. 1 The hoist tower and rubbish chute with storage on the street, illustrating some of the problems associated with working in a city, where there is minimum room.

3.   Organizing the Job Staff

The job superintendent always should request the general contractor's personnel department to provide his job with the best assistants they have for all job positions. A job superintendent must have capable assistants or his job will suffer in terms of both cost and progress. The job superintendent always must instruct his assistants in the methods by which he wants them to operate. He should never permit his assistants to "sink or swim." This is not the way to handle men. It will not take an experienced job superintendent long to find out whether he has good or poor assistants. His first duty is to try to improve the weaker staff members. He must watch them closely, and correct them if and when they are not doing a top-notch job. Assistant superintendents, particularly those working for a job superintendent for the first time, will have to learn how the boss expects them to operate. This is done by absorbing the instructions he gives or by observing how he moves.

4. Choosing the Foremen for the General Contractor and the Subcontractors

If the general contractor is to perform any work on the job (concrete work, bricklaying, carpentry work, excavation, etc.), the job superintendent should request the general contractor's personnel department to supply him with the best foremen available. Foremen are the backbone of the job. They control production and cost. The job superintendent must obtain the cooperation of the foremen, both his own and the subcontractors'. There must be mutual respect between the job staff and the foremen, otherwise the job will not operate as a unit. If the mechanics handled by a foreman are not producing properly, it is the duty of the job superintendent to discuss the matter with the foreman; then a mutual effort can be made to correct the situation. Sometimes cooperation of the union's business agent will have to be solicited.

It is also important that the subcontractors put good foremen on the job. If the job superintendent is not satisfied with the progress or the workmanship of a subcontractor's foreman, he should discuss the matter with the subcontractor himself in an effort to improve the foreman's supervisory efforts. If this fails, the foreman should be replaced. The job superintendent is the boss of the job. He should act like one.

All foremen, whether they work for the general contractor or a subcontractor, must take pride in their mechanics' work. A foreman must guide the mechanics and obtain their respect.

5. Design Placement of Job Shanties

Lay out the shanties or position the trailer as close as possible to the job entrance. Do not put them too close together, because if a fire starts in one shanty it may spread to the others. Always keep fire extinguishers in all shanties, preferably the freeze-proof type.

For the size of job covered in this book, a two-room office trailer and a smaller storage trailer may be sufficient for the general contractor's use. Most furniture comes with the trailer. Additional file cabinets are always required, depending on the particular job requirement.

6.   *Shanties and Facilities for Workmen*

If the general contractor is performing any work on the job (excavation work, concrete work, bricklaying, carpentry, etc.), the job superintendent must provide shanties for the workmen. Trailers are satisfactory for this purpose. Provide places for the workmen's clothes, and furnish good light and heat. The workmen should also have adequate toilet facilities. These can be in the form of one or more chemical toilets, rented from and serviced by a local company. If chemical toilets are not available, a wood frame structure can be built over a large rectangular hole in the ground. This toilet must be kept sanitary by using strong disinfectants or lye.

Shanties or trailers used by the subcontractors should be placed not too far from the job office to allow easy communication.

Electric service must be supplied by the electrical contractor. See Chapter 16.

7.   *Job Staff: Familiarity with Drawings and Specifications*

The job superintendent and his assistant superintendents must study the drawings and specifications continuously. The job staff's major concern is making sure that the job runs efficiently and economically at all times. If they do not know what they are building, they cause disaster.

8.   *Types of Subcontractor Required*

It is of the utmost importance that a job have good subcontractors of proved ability. Good subcontractors help expedite the progress of a job and produce work that does not have to be done again or repaired when the job is completed. Poor subcontractors, on the other hand, are a headache during the course of the job. The main office purchasing department, which selects subcontractors, should also make sure that the top men for the subcontractors have good records for expediting their work. They can dovetail their operations with the general contractor's progress and order their materials and equipment for delivery according to the schedule.

9. *Progress Schedule and Other Lists*
To Be Made Out by Job Staff

Prior to the start of a job, the superintendent should prepare a progress schedule with the completion date based on the date given in the contract. This schedule should be submitted to the person in charge of the job in the main office. The schedule should be in the form of a bar chart or CPM chart showing the starting and completion dates of the job items. A typical list of items is as follows:

1. Wrecking.
2. Site work.
3. Excavation—general.
4. Excavation—footings.
5. Foundation work.
6. Structural frame—concrete or steel (showing progress of each floor).
7. Exterior walls—brick, block, concrete.
8. Interior partitions—possibly by floors.
9. Roofing.
10. Glazing.
11. Carpentry and mill work.
12. Plastering.
13. Floor-finishes, terrazzo, rubber tile, asphalt tile, quarry tile, ceramic tile.
14. Painting.
15. Electrical work.
16. Plumbing.
17. Heating.
18. Air conditioning.
19. Sprinklers.

It should be noted that most contractors set up this schedule in the home office and the job superintendent may comment on its content, but may be required to adhere to it.

The actual progress should be entered weekly for each of these items next to the item that represents the contemplated schedule. This progress schedule will show whether the job is on time or behind. If it is behind schedule, a strong effort must be made to bring progress up to date. This might mean putting on more mechanics, performing the work more efficiently, or making a change in the supervision for any trade falling behind.

The job superintendent, with the help of his assistants, foremen, and subcontractors, must also make out the following lists:

1.   A contract item list may be given to the job superintendent at the start of a project. He must note on this list when each item is required on the job and send the list back to the main office purchasing department, where information is taken from the progress schedule.

2.   Until he gets *written confirmation,* the superintendent must keep a diary in which he records verbal information received from the architects and inspectors and at meetings, as well as unusual items not covered in the daily construction report. It is also good business to make an entry on the page in the diary dated a week in advance of the expiration of the insurance covering each subcontractor.

10.   Job Reports

A written job report shall be made out each day. Every general contractor has his own forms, but basically the information provided on these reports falls into the following categories.

1. Weather and average temperature.
2. The work force of the general contractor and the subcontractors on the site, listing the subcontractor, the trade, the supervisory personnel, and the workmen.
3. Area of work.
4. Material incorporated in the job, such as concrete yardage poured, power equipment installed, and heating, ventilation, and air conditioning (HVAC) installed or delivered.
5. Visitors to the site (architect, engineer, owner).
6. Any comments made by the inspectors affecting the work, including verbal orders that will be confirmed in writing.

7. Any comments that the superintendent may have, such as failure of the home office or the architect to provide requested information, or a subcontractor's poor supervision.

11. Making the Correct Decisions

The job superintendent is like the conductor of a symphony orchestra. He must see that all elements are fitted together at the right time and sequence. The difference is that the job superintendent cannot stage rehearsals. It is important, therefore, that he himself and his assistants be trained to make the proper decisions.

Decisions should never be thought out halfway. There are many ways to solve any problem, and the most expeditious approach must be found. Before giving an order, the superintendents must visualize the outcome of making one decision; then imagine what would happen if another decision were made. After this kind of consideration, a person who is experienced in construction will come up with the right answer. The job superintendent and his assistants simply must be practical thinkers, yet with imagination. An impractical thinker will make mistakes, delay job progress, and run up the job cost. There is no substitute for good, practical, creative thinking. Job staff members must train themselves to do this. One of the most important factors in the chain of events leading to a decision is to make sure that the superintendent and his assistants take care of daily problems.

12. Line and Grade Men

This section contains some key suggestions. Full procedures are detailed in *Construction Measurements,* a volume in this series by Brother B. Austin Barry (Wiley, 1973).

The line and grade men must be the best personnel obtainable. A line and grade crew consists of a party chief (or an assistant superintendent in charge of lines and grades), an instrument man, and two chainmen. On very large projects it may be necessary to have two or more line and grade crews. The job superintendent should go over the line and grade work with each party chief before starting work, to be sure the work is laid out according to the job superintendent's requirements. Since errors by the line and grade crew sometimes are costly to correct, the work must be laid out correctly the first time, then checked. The party chief must satisfy himself before starting that all transits and levels are properly adjusted. These instruments must be checked continually.

To avoid error in running levels, the instrument man must always check back on the bench mark from which he started. Before starting work, bench marks must be established in the most advantageous places: easy to reach and easy to set up over, but safe from traffic. These bench marks must be tied in with the prime bench mark given to the job by the architect.

It is important that the superintendent and his assistants be aware of the location of all these marks. In most instances the superintendent is more familiar with the requirements for future use. He should play an important part in deciding their location.

A bench mark can consist of a steel rod driven into the ground (about 18 to 24 in.), with concrete placed around the rod to a depth of about 18 in. The concrete can also be placed into an augered hole in the ground. Later, the rod is driven into the concrete. After the concrete sets, a level reading is taken on top of the steel rod and recorded. A wooden guard rail about 18 in. high should be placed around the bench mark to make sure that it is not disturbed.

Bench marks can also be placed on the side of adjoining buildings for reference during construction.

To establish building corners and long survey lines, the carpenters install batter boards about 20 to 25 ft from all corners. Two batter boards establish a corner; each one defines a building line, and their intersection establishes a corner. The line and grade crew sets up on each building line and marks it on the batter board with a nail, pencil line, or saw cut. Batter boards are generally made by driving two pointed wood stakes 2 × 4 in. (or 2 × 6 in.) into the ground about 12 in. (or 18 in.) apart. These 2 × 4s (or 2 × 6s) are 4 ft long. They extend above the ground about 3 ft and are set about 3 ft apart. A 1 × 6 (or 2 × 6) is nailed horizontally to the top of the uprights.

It should be noted that the general practice is for the general contractor to hire a licensed surveyor to establish the initial outline of the site, building lines, bench marks, axis lines, and pile layout, if required, as well as any permanent marks used for reference during construction.

During the construction of a reinforced concrete building, the concrete contractor employs his own line and grade crew, and, if the general contractor is doing the work, the concrete superintendent is responsible for the line and grade team.

During the construction of a steel framed building, the steel erector checks the plumbness of the steel with his own crew.

The superintendent, with his own crew, should spot check during the erection of both reinforced concrete and steel framed structures, to ensure that there is no encroachment of adjoining property.

Once the floors have been poured, coordinate lines must be established on each floor. The spacing and location of these working lines is determined by job conditions. When they have been established, the superintendent and his assistants can check out and establish lintel lines, spandrel beam encroachments, and missing floor openings or mistakes. The partition can now be laid out, and the mechanical and electrical contractors have reference points for the piping and equipment layout on each floor.

If the floor elevation is to be brought up to grade by a topping on the arch, a 4 ft bench mark is established on each column above finished grade; this reference mark will be used by all trades to establish the elevation of their work before the finished floor is poured. In a one-story building, with the slab on grade, the 4 ft mark is established as soon as the frame is erected.

13. *Shop Drawings*

Shop drawings are the superintendent's most important tool for the proper erection of the project. Too often, superintendents neglect to review these drawings properly, and embedded items shown on the shop drawings are left out. Such omissions can be very costly.

Most superintendents do not see the shop drawings until they have been reviewed by the home office and approved by the architect or engineer.

14. *Integrated Drawings* (*Coordination Drawing*)

Integrated drawings are required by many specifications. They are prepared by the HVAC contractors. It is a composite drawing indicating the locations of ductwork, defusers, piping, lighting fixtures, and equipment located in the ceilings. Its purpose is to allot space to each of the many systems that must occupy the space between the finished ceiling and the structural floor system above. In its preparation, the ceiling, plumbing, HVAC, and electrical contractors meet several times to coordinate this joint effort. The job superintendent usually becomes involved in the scheduling of these meetings and also attends them. His input is important if it becomes apparent there must be changes in the physical layout of the structure. The integrated drawings are the only shop drawings the superintendent may be involved with during preparations.

Today, with air conditioning a major component in almost all building construction, coordination of the trades is a major concern of the superintendent.

Once the drawings are completed, each representative of the trades involved, sign the drawings, indicating they are in agreement with the space allotted to them. They can then proceed with their individual shop drawings required for their layouts.

Shop drawings for each trade are discussed in the chapters involving the respective trades.

15.   Major Job Responsibilities for a Superintendent or a Project Manager on Cost-Plus Jobs

Controlling Productivity

During any period when productivity from mechanics is low, the job superintendent or project manager must do everything possible to improve production. Low productivity increases building costs to an alarming extent. The job superintendent should study his job to determine the root cause of the low productivity, and find a cure for it.

Cost Studies by the General Contractor

Every two weeks the cost engineer should take off unit costs of excavation, footing forms, wall forms, column forms, floor forms, placing reinforcing steel rods, placing concrete, stripping forms, finishing of concrete slabs, concrete patching and pointing, brick and block laying, and so on, to compare these unit costs with unit costs established by the estimating department. Quantity of materials received should be checked against the estimated materials.

The unit costs should be analyzed by the job superintendent and the foreman of each trade as soon as they are published. Every effort should be made to keep the unit costs within the estimated costs. If the actual costs are running higher than the estimated costs, drastic action should be taken. The supervision may have to be changed, or more economical construction methods tried. Mechanics who are not producing, even after their performance has been discussed with them and with their union business agents, may have to be replaced.

Cost Studies by Subcontractors

The job superintendent should also insist that the subcontractors set up a cost system, which they can review monthly. The job superintendent should be sure that no subcontractor is overrunning his costs.

16.   *Management Requirements of Field Forces: Job Meetings*

During construction, the job superintendent should meet with all his assistant superintendents, job engineers, and representatives of the subcontractors every week or two, to make sure that the job is progressing as a unit and to answer questions about the work. At these meetings unassigned job responsibilities should be allocated. Monthly meetings with the representatives for the architects, structural engineers, and mechanical engineers should be helpful in obtaining missing information and gaining advanced interpretations of the drawings and specifications.

17.   *Responsibilities of Assistants to Job Superintendents*

It is the responsibility of every man on the job staff to perform his duties to the best of his ability. If an assistant is not doing his work properly, he should be so advised by the superintendent. The superintendent should tell the assistant specifically what he is doing wrong, and how to correct it. If the assistant's work does not improve, the superintendent should discuss the matter with the front office. Inefficient assistants will not help complete the job on time, nor within the estimated cost. The job superintendent must detect inefficient supervision, either by his assistants, his foremen, or his subcontractors' men.

18. Job Superintendent Walks the Job

Regardless of how busy a superintendent is, he must walk over all ends of his job, once in the morning and once in late afternoon. He must see personally how the job is progressing, noting on paper operations that are not proceeding properly and acting to correct these deficiencies. There is no substitute for actually observing what is going on. Also, if the rest of the job staff, and the workmen, know that the boss is walking the job twice a day, they will do their best to make a good impression. This should result in increased production. The job superintendent should not make the mistake of walking the job at the same time every day. If the workmen know his routine, they will pace their work accordingly, and a true picture will not be gained. Thus the superintendent should tour at different hours each day, so that no one is expecting him.

19. Assignment of Work for Assistant Superintendents on Large Projects

Each assistant superintendent must be given specific duties to perform. One man should be made responsible for the excavation work, another for checking the form work. The man who has responsibility for the reinforcing steel and concrete placing must compute the concrete yardage required each day and order it. One man must follow all masonry work, plastering, and the "wet" trades. Another man should follow the carpentry work, asphalt, and rubber tile floors. Following the mechanical trades there should be an assistant superintendent, who is thoroughly familiar with mechanical and electrical installations.

On jobs with fewer or efficient assistant superintendents, one man can handle two or three of these items, particularly on the smaller projects. This supervisory force should be large enough to ensure that the work is progressing properly. However the supervisory force should not be so large as to exceed the allowance in the estimate for this item. Too many cooks can gum up the gumbo.

20. *Handling of Job Delays, Changes, and Time Extensions*

Because all jobs generally carry a completion date (which is agreed on with the owner), it becomes important that the job superintendent notify the home office immediately if the job is delayed, specifying who or what is responsible for the delay. Strikes, changes in plans, fires, and union jurisdictional disputes are some potential causes of delay on a job.

As soon as the work resumes on all phases of the job, the superintendent should notify the home office, which will then establish the amount of time lost and its monetary value.

A change order file must be set up. All change orders must be signed either by the owner's representative or by the architect's representative.

Extensions of time should be computed by the job and general superintendents. The contractor's main office should apply to the owner and architect if the extension of time is authentic.

21. *Expediting the Job*

At the start of the job, all subcontractors and material and equipment dealers must be given dates at which the specified materials and equipment are required at the job site. During the course of the work the superintendent and his staff must keep track of these dealers to ensure that their delivery dates can be met. Better still, if the main office has an expediter, much of this follow-up work can be turned over to him. An experienced expediter knows how to handle dealers and manufacturers in trying to obtain scheduled deliveries. If some materials and equipment are behind schedule, the dealer or manufacturer must be watched very closely and prodded. Late delivery of equipment and materials can hold a job back seriously enough to be costly.

During the construction of a project the job superintendent or project manager and the rest of the job staff must work in harmony with the architects, civil and mechanical engineers, inspectors, owners' representatives, and their subcontractors. Arrange meetings with the representatives from time to time to be sure that everyone is working together. Sometimes these meetings unearth serious problems, possibly in the design or construction method of any item. If this happens, take steps to correct the defects.

22.   *Job Superintendent's Obligation to General Contractor*

The superintendent is the field representative for the general contractor. Therefore he should remember that his attitude, if positive and helpful toward his work, the architect, the owner, the public, and others, will do much to give his construction company a bright image. He should be alert and energetic, and should display a desire to cooperate in all his dealings with others. But he should not be put upon. Mature judgment should dictate which items to contest, and to what extent. The job superintendent is responsible for the workmanship, the costs, and the progress during the construction of the project.

23.   *New Materials and Methods*

New material, new equipment, and new methods are always being introduced to improve the cost, strength, architectural appearance, and efficiency of construction on building projects. It is up to the job superintendent, his assistants, and engineers to keep abreast of these developments. This is important, and the requested changes in favor of innovation must be well documented (Figs. 2 and 3).

24.   *Safety*

The superintendent and his staff must be safety minded, to ensure that their job is safe and that all workmen work safely. Hard hats are mandatory: they must be worn on the job at all times by all workmen and visitors. The superintendent should appoint one of his assistants to handle the safety work. The assistant superintendent for safety should work under the direction of the home office's safety engineer, if there is one.

Railings should be installed around all stairways, scaffolds, and so on.

Fig. 2 The superintendent must always be prepared to work with new materials and methods of construction—for example this wood-framed exhibit building at the 1964 New York World's Fair was to be finished in stucco.

Fig. 3 A framed structure covered with a lath, consisting of a kraft-backed paper interwoven with wire mesh nailed to the studding. When the scratch, leveling, and finishing coats were applied, they formed the complete exterior finished wall surface.

Openings in the floor should be covered over substantially, or if the opening is being used, a railing must be placed around the opening with toeboards at the floor level.

While floor forms are being stripped, the stripping area should be roped off to prevent men from walking through it. When stripping close to the outer edge of a building floor, the strippers should be made to work inside a rolling pipe scaffold enclosure. Men have been killed stripping floor forms at the outer edges. Since a stripper could lose his balance and fall when using a long hook to strip spandrel beam forms, a rope might be strung along the outer edge of a floor while the forms are being built and stripped.

The regulations of the Federal Occupational Safety and Health Administration (OSHA) should be studied and followed.

The work area always must be kept clean of scrap lumber, rubbish, and other debris. An untidy job is not a safe job. Workmen should wear safety shoes, or heavy shoes with good thick soles, to prevent nail punctures.

Safety belts should be used by all finishers and window washers working on the outside of the building, and by any other workmen engaged in hazardous work. If men are working above another set of workers, the lower group must be guarded by heavy wood protection. Sometimes a watchman is so stationed that if something falls or is dropped, the observer can warn the workmen by blowing a whistle.

If men are working in trenches in soil that could slide, the sides of the trench must be retained by wood or steel sheet piling. If the soil does not require sheeting, skeleton wood bracing of the banks should be installed.

Substantial railings must be placed on the outside of every scaffold.

25. Room Finish Schedule

It is advantageous to post a card showing the types of materials and finishes required on the floors, walls, ceilings, and other surfaces in every room of the building. All the subcontractors, foremen, and so on, can find out by reading this card how to finish the room, thus eliminating costly errors.

The card should show the room number and name, type of floor, type of base, height and type of wainscot, door numbers and types, type of door saddle, window numbers, whether the windows are to have window guards, type of radiator enclosure, and radiator grille, type of window stool, painting instructions, and other necessary information to finish completely.

26.   *Running the Job*

The following miscellaneous items are essential to the operation of any project and must be dealt with before the job is started.

1. Provide sufficient pay phones around the site that personal phone calls can be made and paid for by the caller.
2. An agreement may be made with a vendor for food-dispensing trucks to visit the job site just before the lunch hour and at coffee breaks, for the convenience of the men.
3. Handling of the payroll today is usually done by the home office. A system of communication with the home office accountant should be established whereby time is called into the office and delivery of the payroll is made promptly. Delay in paying your men creates a very touchy situation, and it is important to maintain good relations with them. Care must be taken for accuracy. No item on a job can affect your goodwill with the men more than a mistake in favor of the company, even an honest mistake, made on someone's paycheck. Each contractor has his own method of payments and dates. This information should be given to the employees on hiring. On large projects payroll departments may be set up on the job site, but this is rare today in most large cities.

Checklist

1. Obtain permits.
2. Establish access to site.
3. Contact Traffic Department for "No Parking" signs (if required).
4. Erect construction fence.
5. Locate job offices.
6. Locate temporary toilets.
7. Check conditions of existing buildings.
8. Establish bench marks and survey lines.
9. Bring in temporary water and power.

2

Excavation, Pile Foundations, and Dewatering

1. Excavation

The first major operation in new construction is excavation. Every job has its own problems, and this is one area that must receive the job superintendent's full attention. If an assistant superintendent is available, he should be assigned to stay with the excavating contractor at all times. If no assistant is available, a qualified laborer from your company should be assigned to stay with any machine operator working on the excavation. Since the equipment operator usually cannot see into the bottom of the excavation at all times, your man's job is to watch for any underground utilities that may be encountered.

Before starting excavation, or performing any work that might endanger the stability of adjacent structures, the following information about these adjacent structures must be obtained:

Foundation elevations.

Character of soil on which the structures stand.

Existence of party walls on which the adjacent structures may depend.

General condition of adjacent structures. Look for settlement or other cracks in floors and walls; record or photograph them, and show the evidence to the owners of the adjacent structures.

Study the plans of the adjacent structures if they are available or filed in the building department.

It may be necessary to dig exploration pits within the area of the new building. These pits should be carried not lower than the proposed foundations for the new building and alongside of the adjacent structures. Take adequate soil samples for lab testing.

In some localities the owner of the adjacent buildings is held responsible for maintaining his own structure. If this is not covered by the local building code, the services of a well-established underpinning contractor should be sought to make the adjacent structures safe. The owners of these structures should be given details of how this work will be carried on.

2. Access to Site

Before starting to excavate for the building, the excavation contractor should level the entire site to an elevation designated as the bottom of the road stone or gravel base, for permanent roads. For nonroad area, level to the bottom of the new topsoil, if good topsoil is present on the site. Next, place the crushed stone or gravel base for the permanent site roads. Additional crushed stone or gravel roads (access roads) should be installed from the permanent road lines to the building site, brick and tile storage areas, reinforcing steel storage and fabrication yards, lumber storage, and form building yards, and to the hoist towers. Too many superintendents make the mistake of building access roads that will not last throughout the job. When this important detail is neglected, everyone on the job has to plod through mud after every rain or snow storm, for the duration of the work. Trucks break down trying to run in mud, and bulldozers must pull or push them through it to reach their destinations. This is a costly procedure.

The crushed stone or gravel base for new permanent roads must be built according to the specifications, so why not take advantage of this road base during the construction period? Always keep the mud and debris cleaned off this base, by using either a road scraper or a street-sweeping power broom. After the mud has been removed, the crushed stone base should be worked with a road grader to keep a good crown for drainage, when the crushed stone base is first installed. Crushed stone screening should be swept into the voids of the crushed stone, to assure good drainage and to keep as much rainwater or snow as possible from seeping through the road base, thus softening the subgrade.

3. *General Excavation for the Building*

The job superintendent should ensure that the excavation contractor has good and fairly new equipment, and that the excavator services and maintains his equipment daily. See *Construction Equipment Guide,* by D. A. Day (Wiley 1973). Broken-down equipment delays a job, hinders progress, and costs money. Prior to actual excavation, the line and grade men should lay out the buildings, place building lines on the batter boards, and instruct the excavator how deep to cut. Sometimes the grade at the bottom of the excavation is lowered accordingly. This allows the footing excavation waste to be spread among the footings, so that it does not have to be hauled out of the excavation. This additional fill should be tamped down by kneading movement of equipment and workmen, working in the excavation (Fig. 4).

If water occurs in the excavation, it must be pumped out to keep the hole dry. Sometimes underfloor drains are installed and covered with porous backfill. Underfloor drains are generally installed just before the basement floor is to be poured.

Fig. 4   Hand tamping backfill with the use of a machine tamper.

4. Securing Excavation Sidewalls

Figure 5 shows how to shore excavation banks, when this is required. Shoring keeps the soil outer excavation walls in place and out of the hole.

As the excavation is completed in part of the hole, the line and grade men lay out the footings. Here again, batter boards are used to define the footing locations in both directions. The footings are then excavated, generally by hand. If they are large, however, a backhoe or front-end loader is used.

The excavator must work closely with the concrete contractor once the excavation has reached the desired grade. Care must be taken not to pile excavated material in the way of access for pouring concrete. This can be a major problem on small sites with interior footings.

On large construction sites it may become necessary to build ramps into the hole. The economics of the site will determine whether a timber ramp is built, or, as in most cases, a ramp is built with the excavated material or, borrowed fill; if the former is not suitable.

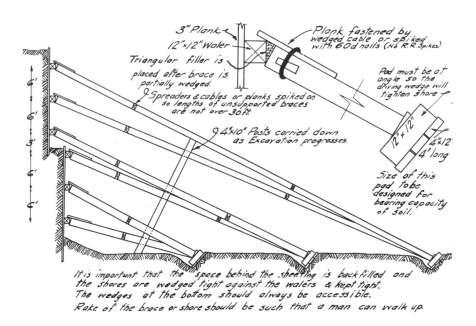

Fig. 5 Typical method for sheeting and shoring.

5. Computing Excavated Material

If the contract calls for the contractor to be paid for excavated material by the yard, the quantities paid for are calculated from in-place material, with no allowance for overcut. The unit price has in it an allowance for overcut, but this may not be that accurate; therefore all efforts must be taken to keep the overcut at a minimum.

Most unit price contracts have different classifications of excavated material. Some of the classifications are listed below:

Stripping top soil.
General excavation—left on site, for backfill.
General excavation—hauled away.
General excavation—rock.
Trenching for utilities.
Porous fill.
Hand excavation.
Borrowed fill.
Backfill—not compacted.
Backfill—compacted.

A separate contract price is established in the excavation contractor's subcontract for each of the foregoing items, sometimes on a square foot basis, but generally on a cubic yard basis.

6. Pile Foundations

Piles: End-Bearing and Friction, Precast, and Poured-in-Place

On some projects the rock is so far below excavation grade that to excavate to that depth would be too costly. If the earth will not carry the design load, piles must be driven. There are two classes of piles: end-bearing, and friction. Both these types can be precast, or poured in place if they are concrete. They may also be steel.

The end-bearing pile is generally driven to rock or hard earth and acts as a column that supports the building on rock or hard pan, whereas the friction pile depends on friction between a corrugated tapered pile shell filled with concrete, or a tapered precast pile, and the surrounding earth.

After the friction pile has been driven, a load test is placed on the pile to determine whether it will support the design load. If so, the other piles are driven to that depth. If the pile settles under the load test, the pile must be driven further. Besides steel "H" columns, there are three types of pile in each class: creosoted wood pile; precast concrete pile, which is poured in a shop or on the job and must be moist cured for 28 days before it can be driven; and poured-in-place concrete pile. The third type consists of a corrugated sheet-metal tapered shell casing that is placed around a solid metal mandrel. The mandrel with the corrugated sheet-metal casing is driven either to rock or to a depth where it "sets up" when the friction valve between the earth and the pile meets the specification required to carry the design load. The mandrel is then withdrawn by the pile driver, and the pile shell is filled with concrete.

Driving Piles

Drive piles with a pile driver, which consists of a crane and a set of hanging leads secured to the top of the crane boom. The pile-driving mechanism slides in the hanging leads while the piles are being driven.

This mechanism is either a single-acting pile driver or a vibratory motor. In the single-acting pile driver the mechanism consists of a heavy metal weight sliding in the hanging leads and secured to the drum of the crane by a steel cable. The pile is placed between the hanging leads by means of a steel cable secured to a second drum on the crane, and it is hammered into the ground by the weight, which is free falling. As soon as the weight strikes the pile, the crane operator lifts the weight to the top of the leads for another free drop.

The double-acting pile driver mechanism has a piston operating in a cast steel container. The piston is operated either by steam or by compressed air. The pile is placed in the leads under the double-acting piston mechanism. Steam or air is then turned on in the same manner as railroad steam engine functions. This gives the driver many blows per minute.

In driving piles the crew must be careful not to destroy the bottom of the pile after the pile has hit bed rock. If the pile is crushed against the rock by too much driving, the full value of the end bearing is destroyed. The structural engineer sets up a specification stating the maximum number of blows per time unit that a pile should receive. This specification must be followed.

The engineer may specify that the first friction pile be load tested after driving, to be sure that the pile will not settle under the weight of the design load.

7. Caissons

If the ground on which a building is to be constructed is a dump and contains material through which a pile cannot be driven, steel caissons are substituted. Caissons are composed of heavy metal sheets about 4 to 5 ft wide. Bent into a circle having a diameter of about 2 ft, 8 in., tops of metal caisson sections are reinforced with heavy angles secured to the caisson sheets with rivets, welds, or bolts. One angle is placed at the top of the caisson section and one angle at the bottom, for securing the sections together. Punch holes in the outstanding legs of the angles, and insert bolts to hold the sections in place. Put additional angles around the caisson section to stiffen it. All angles are inside the caisson sections, to prevent them from hanging up on the adjoining earth as the caisson is lowered.

To start caisson operations, dig a hole in the ground slightly larger than the caisson diameter. Then lower the first caisson section into this hole and partially backfill, removing the ground inside the caisson by hand. The earth under the caisson lining itself has to be removed by hand to allow the caisson to continue down. The first caisson section is then pounded down to about the level of the surrounding ground, then another section added and excavation continues.

A discussion of pile and caisson construction may be found in Gordon Fletcher and Al Smoots, *Construction Guide for Soils and Foundations* (Wiley 1974).

8. Dewatering

When the foundation extends below the water table it is necessary to dry out the hole. The method used to overcome the problem varies, depending on the soil conditions.

Coffer dams may be used for the construction of bridges and piers;

Fig. 6 A test pit is dug in the middle of the excavation to observe the lowering of the water level by the well point system. The excavation must go down 15 ft more.

sheet piling and direct pumping are effective where the percolation is slow. In sandy soil a well point system may be used. Figure 6 shows a test pit during dewatering by a well point system.

Dewatering is a very special field, and when problems develop, it is best to call in a specialist. Where the water condition is a major factor in the construction, the home office contracts out the work and the superintendent's only function is to supervise and assist the subcontractor in the performance of his work.

At times, however, the superintendent must cope with local water conditions. Most local water conditions are due to surface runoff and there is usually a simple solution. The water should be intercepted at the source and channeled away from the foundation construction. A ditch may be dug, sometimes filled with gravel, and sloped to a low point. The water is then pumped out of the hole. Another method is to overcut the area 6 to 12 in. and backfill with gravel. This provides a drainage area to channel the water to a low point, where it can be pumped out. It also provides a dry area for the men to work on. When only several feet of water is encountered in a restricted area, the hole can usually be pumped out directly. The sides of the excavation should be sheeted.

The superintendent should always check the boring logs for indications of the water table. They are his most reliable information before excavating. Armed with this knowledge, he is then prepared to cope with any condition that is encountered. It is very common for the water table to vary during the year. Thus the superintendent should note the time of the year the boring logs were taken. During the spring the water table in most regions may be higher than it is in the winter. *Construction Dewatering Guide,* by J. P. Powers (Wiley, to be published) can be consulted.

Checklist

1. Check boring logs.
2. Establish access.
3. Lay out batter boards.
4. Provide for the public safety.
5. Establish whether sheeting is required.
6. Check elevations and locations.
7. Provide access for concrete.
8. Check backfill compaction requirements.

3

Concrete

1. Design and Tests

Before the concrete can be poured, most specifications call for a design mix to be approved by the engineer. This document is usually submitted as soon as the contract is awarded by the home office, and the superintendent should be aware of its status. Having an open excavation waiting for the design mix to be approved is something one does not want.

Concrete, when poured, must be sampled and sent to a testing laboratory for strength tests. If a testing lab is employed to make field samples the only responsibilities of the superintendent are to see that the lab is properly informed when its services are needed and to provide storage on the job for the test cylinders until they are picked up. When no testing lab personnel are employed to carry out the field sampling and testing, it falls on the Superintendent to see that the necessary test cylinders are on the job, as well as the slump cones and the test equipment for checking air entrained concrete, if called for. All tests are simple to make, and the superintendent or his assistant makes them.

A testing lab is employed to break the cylinders at 7 and 28 days and submit the report, through the home office, to the engineer. The job specifications indicate how many test cylinders are required for each pour. They also indicate the maximum slump and air entrainment required (See Portland Cement Association Bulletins).

2. Fundamental Facts About Concrete

In properly made concrete, each particle or aggregate must be surrounded by cement paste, and all spaces between the particles must be filled with paste, not air. This means that the concrete must be mixed long enough for this condition to exist. The aggregates are inert material, and the paste (composed of cement and water in specified amounts) is the cementing medium. The paste binds the aggregate into a solid mass. Thus the quality of the concrete depends on the strength, durability, and resistance to the passage of water of the cement paste.

Resistance to Freezing and Thawing

The important uses of concrete are in structures and pavements, which are expected to have long life, with minimum maintenance. Concrete must have good resistance to exposure. If the paste in concrete contains little water, the concrete will be more resistant to freezing and thawing than concrete whose paste has a high water content.

Impermeable Concrete

On many structures it is important for the concrete to be watertight. Tests show that mortar (paste) cured moist for 7 days had no leakage when mixed with 5.6 gallons of water per standard bag of cement.

Strength of Concrete

The compressive strength of concrete decreases with increase of mixing water. Also tensile, flexural, and bond strengths increase with age.

Moist Curing and the Effect of Temperatures

Strength will grow with age as long as the concrete is prevented from drying out. Concrete must be kept moist as long as possible. Concrete cured under higher temperature conditions will gain strength faster. At optimum, concrete should be moist cured at about 72°F.

Materials for Concrete

PORTLAND CEMENT.   There are eight main types of Portland cement.

1.   *Type I, Normal Portland Cement.*   This material is to be used for all concrete that is not subject to special sulfate hazards, or where the heat

generated by the hydration of the cement will not cause an objectionable rise in temperature.

2. *Type II, Modified Portland Cement.* This cement has a lower heat of hydration than type I and generates heat at a slower rate. It is used in large piers, heavy abutments, and heavy retaining walls, or when the concrete is placed in warm weather.

3. *Type III, High Early Strength Portland Cement.* This cement is used where the schedule does not permit normal time for in-place curing.

4. *Type IV, Low Heat Portland Cement.* This cement is used where the amount and rate of heat generated must be kept to a minimum, for example, in large masses of concrete such as are found in gravity dams.

5. *Type V, Sulfate-Resistant Portland Cement.* This cement, used in structures exposed to sulfate action, is employed in western states where soils and water have a high alkali content.

6. *Air-Entrained Portland Cement.* This cement is used to produce concrete that is resistant to frost action and to protect the concrete from the effects of calcium chloride applications for melting snow and ice. Air-entrained cement is used in concrete roads, shipping platforms, sidewalks, and so on, where salt or calcium chloride is applied to keep the pavements clear of frost materials.

7. *White Portland Cement.* Used to contrast color, staining, or darkening of concrete, this cement is also employed for decorative purposes; it offers an "all-white" structure.

8. *Waterproof Portland Cement.* This material is used to harden concrete at high temperatures or wet conditions such as those prevailing in deep wells and other places that must be kept dry.

All cement must be stored in a dry place and *kept* dry. Do not attempt to store too much cement, because if any moisture reaches the powder, the strength will be drastically reduced. Besides, it becomes costly to keep much cement dry, and it requires too much space.

Water used for concrete must be free from acids, alkalis, oil, decaying vegetable matter, and all other foreign substances.

AGGREGATES. Aggregates should consist of clean, hard, strong, and durable particles, all free from chemicals or coatings of clay or other fine material. Dirt, silt, clay, coal, mica, salts, humus, or other organic matter are the contaminating materials most often encountered in aggregates.

These must be removed before aggregates can be used in concrete. Weak, friable, or laminated particles are not to be used as aggregates. Shale, stones laminated with shale, and most cherts must also be avoided.

The most commonly used aggregates are clean sand, gravel, and crushed stone. Cinders are sometimes used for cinder concrete fill. Sharp, angular, and rough aggregate particles, or flat and elongated particles require more fine material to produce workable concrete mixtures than do rounded aggregate particles. The grading of aggregates is determined by sieve analysis specified by ASTM or AASHO.* Standard sieves for fine aggregate are numbers 4, 8, 16, 30, 50 and 100; coarse aggregates require the following sieves: 6, 3, 1½, ¾, and ⅜ in., and number 4.

Fineness modulus is used as an index to the fineness or coarseness of aggregates. Fineness modulus is the sum of the cumulative percentages of the aggregates retained on the standard sieves, divided by 100.

3.   *Pouring Concrete: General*

Before the first yard of concrete is poured, the work area must be established for bending of the reinforcing rods (or storage area, if they come bent), an area for the carpenters to fabricate forms, and a storage yard for material. These are locations established in conjunction with the concrete contractor.

Today most concrete comes from "ready-mix" plants. It is important to provide easy access for the trucks, as well as parking space for the waiting trucks, in the street or on the site.

Pouring concrete for each job and operation requires a special operation. The following are some methods used under different conditions. We have gone into much detail because the general contractor may undertake this phase of the work with his own forces.

To place concrete into footings, pile caps, or grade beams when the excavation is deep, some contractors set up a metal or wood concrete hopper, holding several yards of concrete in the hole at the edge of the excavation. A wood or metal concrete chute is built with one end in the hopper and the other mounted on a carpenter's horse, or wood blocks on

---

* See Appendix for a listing of industry standards.

the top of the bank. The ready-mix concrete trucks dump the concrete into the concrete chute, filling the hopper below. The concrete is then wheeled from the hopper to the form in concrete buggies moving on rubber-tired wheels, either pushed by hand or motor driven for ease. The buggies are wheeled on wooden concrete runway panels. These panels are made by placing three 2 x 6 rough lumber planks, 13 ft long, on a work bench. Rough 1 x 4s about 3 ft 8 in. or 4 ft long are nailed at right angles to the three 2 x 6s, which are laid flat on the bench. Place one 2 x 6 at the middle of the run panel, and nail the other two about 1 or 2 in. in from the ends of the 1 x 4 boards. Then nail the 1 x 4 boards to the three 2 x 6s about ½ in. apart; this leaves a space through which concrete drippings can fall, so that they do not collect on the run panels. These panels are made up at the start of a job and are used for all concrete placing, including floors, columns, and so on. Figures 7–9 give form sketches for footings.

If there is a crane on the job, and the excavated area is large, the concrete hopper in the excavation can be placed some distance from the side of the excavation, and the crane, working in the excavation, can swing the concrete by means of a bottom-drop, 1.0 cubic yard, concrete hopper bucket, from the concrete trucks on the original ground to the concrete hopper in the excavation. This method will save some distance of wheeling concrete. Since crane rental is costly, however, a crane is not used unless it has to be on the job for other purposes. Sometimes the crane drops the concrete directly into the footings or pile caps. This method is not recommended, since the force of a large volume of concrete being dropped into a form increases the pressure on the form, possibly causing collapse. Figure 10 illustrates one method of pouring foundations.

4. *Pouring Concrete for Structural Steel and Reinforced Concrete Buildings; Fireproofing a Structural Steel Building*

As soon as the structural steel columns, beams, and girders for the floor system have been erected on two or three floors, plank over the upper floor and start to form for the steel column fireproofing. While the structural steel is being erected, make up the column panels. These panels are made up, one for each of the four sides of the column, to a length reaching

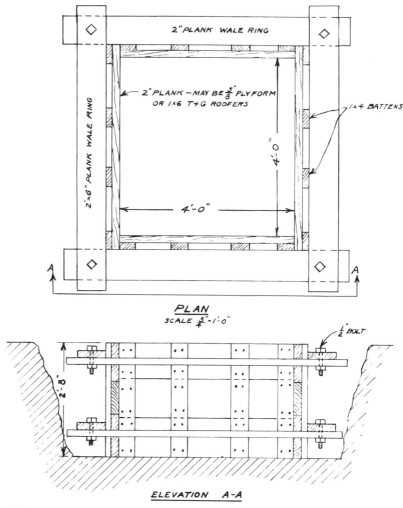

PLAN
SCALE ¾"=1'-0"

ELEVATION A-A

NOTE :- NUMBER OF WALE RINGS REQUIRED DEPENDS ON DEPTH OF FOOTING.
NUMBER OF BATTENS AND WIDTH OF WALES INCREASES FOR LARGE FOOTINGS.

Fig. 7 Individual flat column footing form.

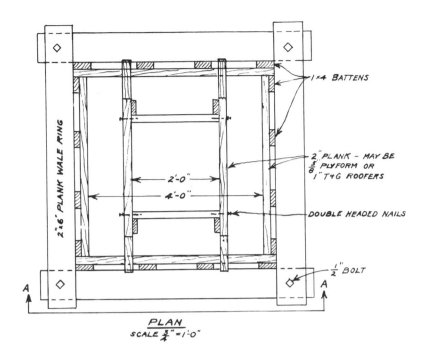

2"x6" PLANK WALE RING

1"x4 BATTENS

2" PLANK - MAY BE
⅝" PLYFORM OR
1" T&G ROOFERS

DOUBLE HEADED NAILS

2'-0"

4'-0"

½" BOLT

A   A

PLAN
SCALE ¾" = 1'-0"

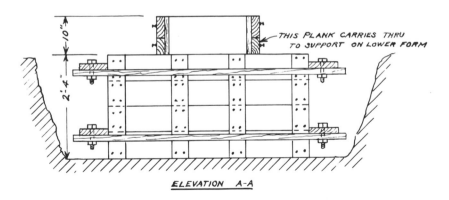

10"

2'-4"

THIS PLANK CARRIES THRU
TO SUPPORT ON LOWER FORM

ELEVATION A-A

Fig. 8 Individual flat column stepped column footing form.

SKETCH #3 — DEEP FOOTING FORM

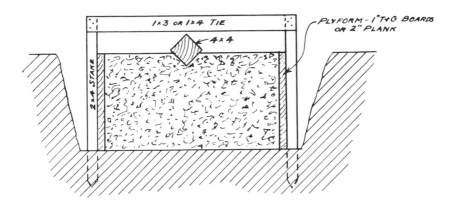

SKETCH #4 — STEEL FORMS

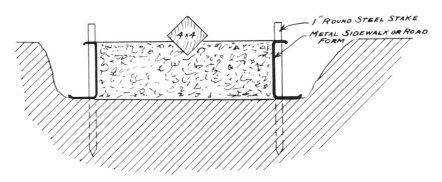

Fig. 9 Simple wall footings.

from the top of the footings to the bottom of the floor slab, with cutout for the fireproofing forms for the beams and girders that frame into the column. Reinforcing goes in before the first three column form panels are placed around the column. After the reinforcing steel hoops, and so on, have been installed, put the electrical boxes and the conduit, plumbing, and heating pipes into position. The whole column form is then closed with the fourth panel. Metal hinged column clamps (which come in two sections) are wrapped around the column form. These column clamps

Fig. 10 Preparation of underground pump house foundation. At one end, the lathers are placing the reinforcing, the plumbers, piping, and the electricians, conduits. At the far end the balance of the work slab is being poured. The work slab will be covered with membrane waterproofing as a protection coat, before the trades work on it. The waterproofing forms an envelope with the waterproofing going up the wall. The building will be submerged in 20 ft of water. Note the well point system around the perimeter of the excavation.

are spaced closer at the bottom of the column because as the column is being poured (and until the concrete sets up) the concrete exerts more pressure on the lower third of the column form. Wooden blocks placed against the bottom of each column panel side are nailed to the concrete floor with concrete nails. This holds the extreme bottom end of the column form in place. Space the metal column clamps farther apart in the middle third of the column form, and still farther apart in the upper third. The same procedure is followed in building up forms for concrete columns.

The exterior walls for a structural steel or concrete building are generally poured after the exterior columns have been built. Place bond bars into two sides of the column form to tie the wall into the exterior columns. A beveled wood keyway is also nailed to the same sides of the column form with the bond bars, also to tie in the walls.

If the column fireproofing on a steel building is to be poured in advance of the floors, concrete run panels are placed on top of the steel beams and girders. Then the concrete is wheeled from a receiving hopper holding about 1.5 cubic yards or concrete; this is bolted to the hoist tower legs, and into it the concrete is dumped from the concrete bucket on the holding about 1.5 cubic yards of concrete; this is bolted to the hoist tower buggy, or a gasoline-powered buggy. Several columns are filled simultaneously, instead of one at a time. This procedure is easier on the column form, if it is not filled up too quickly.

Electric concrete vibrators, operated either by a motor generator set or by temporary electric power, are used to compact the concrete in the columns. This prevents honeycomb from forming on the concrete surface. If the concrete column face is to be exposed, ¾ in. wood chamfer strips are nailed to each column corner in the form, to prevent chipping the right angle corner.

To assure a hard, shiny surface that will take a good paint job, the forms on all concrete faces should not be stripped for 7 days. Then do a minimum of painting and rubbing. If the forms are stripped earlier, and the surface rubbed, a sandy surface finish that will not take a good paint job will result. The same theory applies to poured concrete buildings. Some steel and concrete forms appear in Figs. 11–15.

5. *Placing of Concrete*

The method of handling and moving concrete from the mixer or receiving hopper to the point of placing in forms is very important. The concrete should be placed into the form as close as possible to its final position. It should not be allowed to run or be pushed by vibrators, paddles, and so on, for any long distance in the form. Running or pushing results in segregation of the mortar, sand, and the coarse aggregates. Concrete should be placed in horizontal layers of fairly uniform thickness.

In high walls, concrete should not drop freely more than 4 or 5 ft. The high walls should be filled to within 12 or 18 in. of the top, and a short time allowed for the concrete to settle but not set. Complete pouring the wall with a stiffer mix.

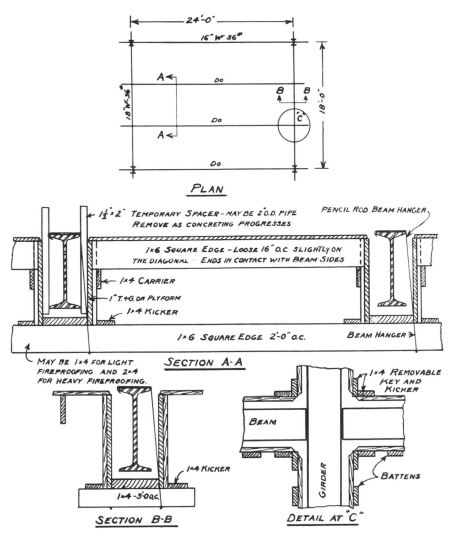

Fig. 11 Floor forms—structural steel frame, fireproofed.

In narrow walls with much reinforcing steel, place wood or metal receiving hoppers at intervals along the wall. Lengths of rubber or canvas elephant-trunk-type chutes should be attached to the bottom of these hoppers. The concrete, flowing through this type of chute from the hoppers, will not strike the reinforcing steel rods; thus segregation is prevented.

For wide walls, place metal receiving hoppers with round discharge

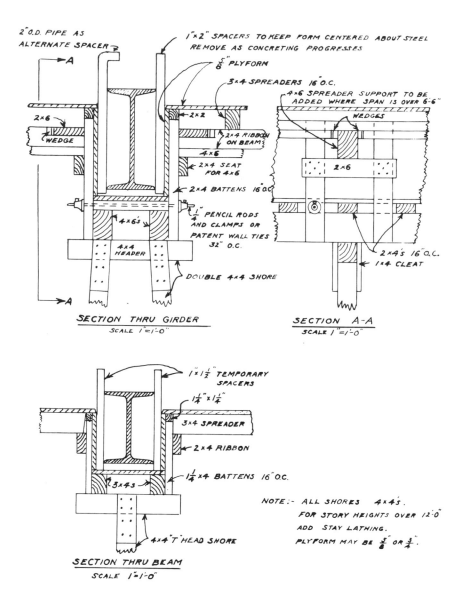

Fig. 12 Floor forms—fireproofing steel beams and girders.

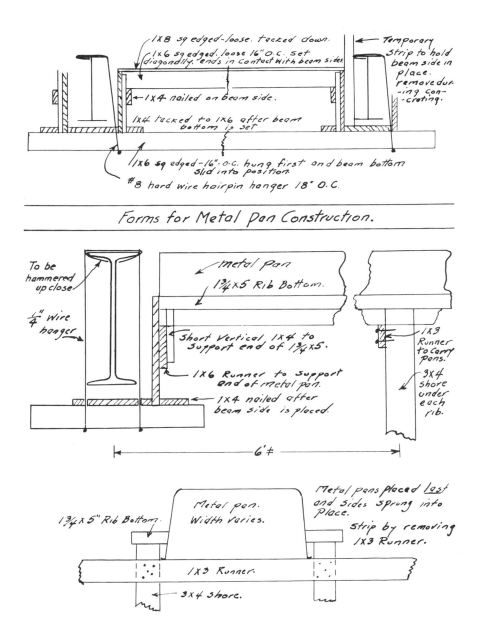

1X8 sq edged-loose. tacked down.

1x6 sq edged. loose 16" O.C. Set diagondlly. ends in Contact With beam sides.

Temporary Strip to hold beam side in place. remove during con-creting.

1X4 nailed on beam side.

1x4 tacked to 1x6 after beam bottom is set

1X6 sq edged-16"-O.C. hung first and beam bottom Slid into position.

#8 hard wire hairpin hanger 18° O.C.

Forms for Metal Pan Construction.

To be hammered up close

¼" wire hanger

metal Pan

1¾X5 Rib Bottom.

Short Vertical 1x4 to support end of 1¾x5.

1X6 Runner to support end of metal pan.

1X4 nailed after beam side is placed.

1X3 Runner to Carry Pans.

3X4 shore under each rib.

6'±

Metal pan. Width varies.

1¾ x 5" Rib Bottom.

Metal pans placed last and sides sprung into place.

Strip by removing 1X3 Runner.

1X3 Runner.

3X4 Shore.

Fig. 13 Typical forms for light concrete arches and fireproofing structural steel.

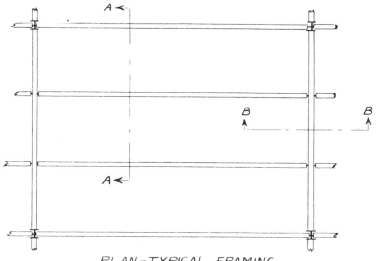

PLAN-TYPICAL FRAMING

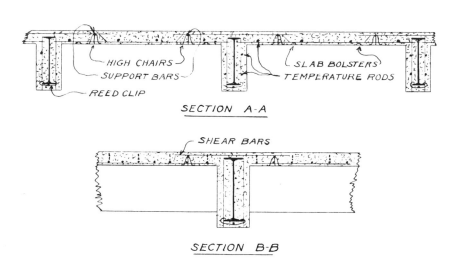

HIGH CHAIRS
SUPPORT BARS
REED CLIP
SLAB BOLSTERS
TEMPERATURE RODS

SECTION A-A

SHEAR BARS

SECTION B-B

Fig. 14 Structural steel–fireproofed.

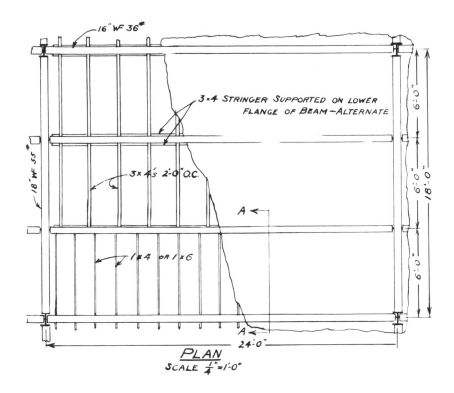

16" WF 36#

3×4 STRINGER SUPPORTED ON LOWER
FLANGE OF BEAM—ALTERNATE

3×4's 2'-0" O.C.

18" WF 55#

A

1×4 OR 1×6

6'-0"

6'-0"   18'-0"

6'-0"

A

24'-0"

PLAN
SCALE 1/4" = 1'-0"

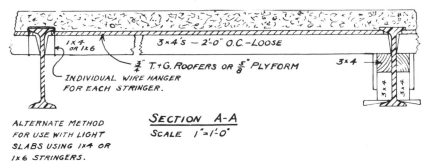

1×4
OR 1×6

3×4's — 2'-0" O.C.—LOOSE

3/4" T.+G. ROOFERS OR 5/8" PLYFORM

3×4

INDIVIDUAL WIRE HANGER
FOR EACH STRINGER.

3×4   3×4

ALTERNATE METHOD
FOR USE WITH LIGHT
SLABS USING 1×4 OR
1×6 STRINGERS.

SECTION A-A
SCALE 1" = 1'-0"

Fig. 15 Floor forms—structural steel frame, not fireproofed.

bottom openings at intervals along the wall top. Attach flexible metal drop chutes to the hopper bottoms by means of short chains (which are slipped over two hooks attached to the hopper bottoms). The steel drop chutes are made in short sections and are secured to each other by short chains. Two hooks are attached to the bottom of each section of chute. Remove the bottom sections of these chutes as the concrete rises in the wall.

In pouring floor slabs, concrete placing should start at the point farthest from the source of concrete (hoist towers or receiving hoppers). Each buggy load or batch of concrete should be dumped against the concrete batch previously placed. The concrete is then screeded off. This method produces a more compact floor slab.

To eliminate segregation when using receiving hoppers, the discharge should be in the center of the hopper.

Chutes for placing concrete should have round bottoms and should be large enough to prevent overflow. Chutes should be put on a slope not flatter than 1–3, and not steeper than 1–2. Chutes should have a receiving hopper at the charging end and a baffle board at the bottom end, which forces the concrete to drop vertically, thus preventing segregation.

Before pouring walls situated on top of other concrete, place a layer of 1–3 cement and sand grout over the concrete in place to a depth of about 2 in. This grout mixes with the new concrete and provides a good bond with no honeycomb at the bottom of the wall.

Concrete walls must be cured. Perforated garden hose should be placed on top of the wall to allow the water from the perforations to spill over the sides of the wall. Sometimes burlap bags, sewed together, are draped over the sides of the wall, then continually kept wet.

6. *Wall Forms*

Before plywood sheets are cut and used for forms, they should be dipped in form oil. You can rent or buy a metal tank, about 8½ ft long, 4½ ft high and about 8 in. wide, for this purpose. A wood box built to these inside dimensions also can be used, if the inside joints in the boards or plywood are sealed. The form oil is poured into the tank up to the 4 ft mark, then the plywood is dipped into the oil bath by using surrounding slings. After dipping, the plywood should be allowed to dry on a wooden rack for a day or two, depending on local humidity.

Wall forms are generally built with 4 x 8 ft plywood panels, 2 x 4 studs, spaced 14 in. apart, are toe nailed into a 2 x 4 or 2 x 6, nailed to the concrete floor. Figure 16 shows carpenters working on wall forms, and Fig. 17 shows work areas inside a sheeted pit.

If 3 x 4 studs are used, the spacing can be made wider. The plywood is then nailed to the 2 x 4 studs, but not too rigidly, and 1 x 4 wood cleats are nailed to the studs to carry the walers while they are being installed. The form for the other side of the wall is positioned after the reinforcing rods have been placed. If the wall is not thick, this side can be prefabricated. Walers that consist of two 2 x 4s, with the 4 in. side horizontal, are prefabricated by nailing them together with a ¾ in. block between the two 2 x 4s. Then holes are drilled between the two 2 x 4s of the waler and also through the plywood, on both sides of the wall form, so that the wall ties will slide through the forms on both wall sides.

Fig. 16 Carpenters' work area and forming up the walls with reinforcing in place.

Fig. 17 Working inside a sheeted pit. The sheeting remains in place and becomes the form for the concrete wall.

On a wall about 10 ft high, the walers and form ties are spaced about 6 in. from the bottom of the wall. The next walers above are spaced at 10 in. apart. The third set of walers are spaced at 14 in. apart, the fourth at 16 in. apart, and all walers above at 18 in. apart.

Small cast-metal wedges (cast in a slight curve, with a slot in the middle) are slipped over the both ends of the wall tie. Ties have a button on each end, against which one side of the tie rests. The other end of the wedge rests against the waler. The wedges are purchased with the wall ties (two wedges required for each tie).

In stripping the wall forms, the tie wedges are removed first, then the walers, followed by the studs, then the plywood. Both ends of the wall ties are twisted until they break off, an inch or so back from the face of the wall. The wall ties have a pinched section near each end, which makes it easier to break off the tie. Fill these holes in the wall with a cement and sand grout, of the same mix as the mortar in the wall. The wedges are recovered and reused, while the wall tie stays embedded in the wall.

On walls placed monolithic with the floor, a 2 x 10 ledger board is nailed to the 2 x 4 wall studs to support the 3 x 4 floor form joists. On the opposite side of the wall form at the floor line, a wood bracket is installed to keep the wall form from spreading while it is filling. This bracket is formed by nailing a 2 x 4 to the 2 x 4 wall studs. The 2 x 4s are supported with 1 x 4 diagonal braces on top and bottom of the 2 x 4, nailed to the 2 x 4 studs. A 1 x 4 runner piece is nailed to the extreme outside edges of the horizontal 2 x 4s, to keep them in line. Sketches of various wall forms appear in Figs. 18–23.

7.   *Column Forms and Methods of Placing Concrete*

The four side panels of the column form are fabricated in the form yard. These panels are generally built of ¾ in. plywood, or tongue and groove boards tied together with 2 x 4, 3 x 4, or 4 x 4 planks. Vertical members are spaced about 8 in. apart. When the column reinforcing steel rods and ties are in position, three of the side panels are situated. The electric receptacles, conduit, piping, and heating pipes are installed, and the fourth panel is then put into position. Metal column clamps are placed around the completed column forms, beginning about 8 in. from the bottom of the column. The next clamp goes 14 in. above the first clamp, the third about 24 in. above the second, and the rest are spaced about 30 in. apart going up.

The columns should be poured the day before the floor is poured. If the columns are so placed ahead of the floor and then stripped, ⅝ or ¾ in. bolts can be placed, two on each side of the column form, before it is poured. After the columns have been stripped, 3 x 4s or 4 x 4s (each the length of the column face) are bolted to these bolts, to carry the floor form joists. The bolts protrude from the face of the concrete column about 6 in. and have a threaded exposed end that takes a nut.

Metal column forms are also available. These can be rented. This type of column form is generally used for columns supporting a flat slab floor. Metal column forms have metal column clamps or rings spaced at various intervals to prevent the form from spreading while being concreted. This

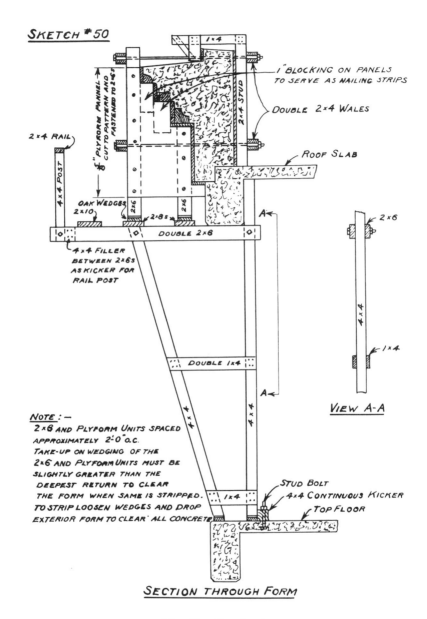

Fig. 18 Cornice forms.

48

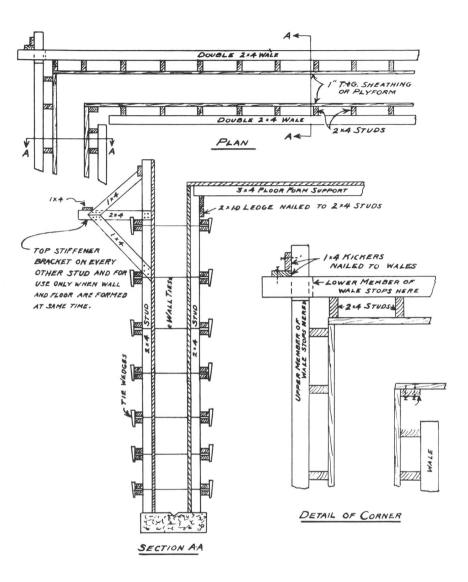

Fig. 19 Wall forms—ordinary basement walls.

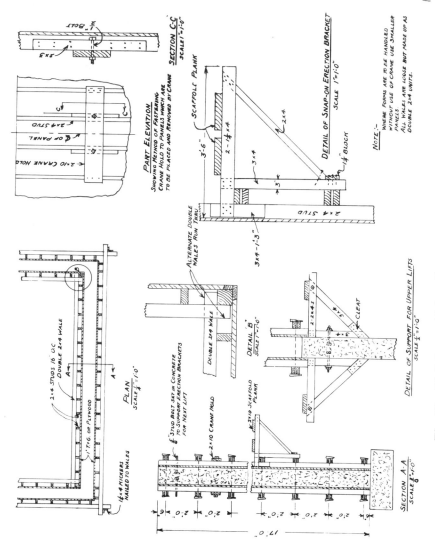

Fig. 20 Wall forms—high walls concreted in two or more lifts.

50

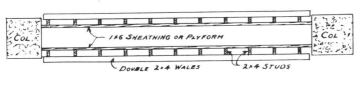

PLAN

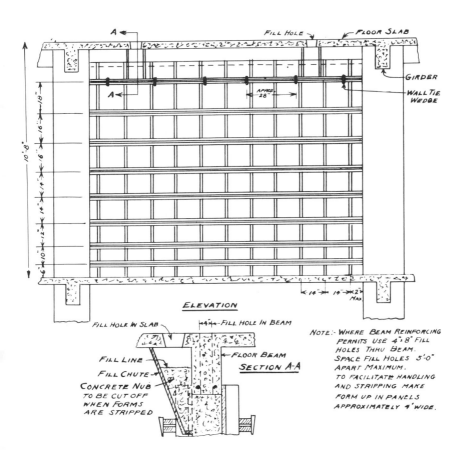

ELEVATION

Fig. 21 Wall forms—partition walls placed after floors.

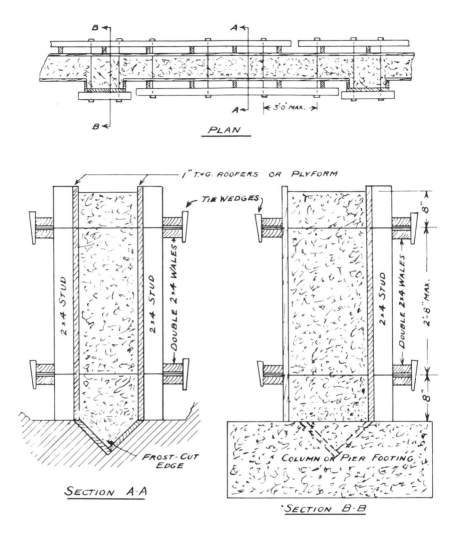

Fig. 22 Wall forms—grade walls designed as beams.

52

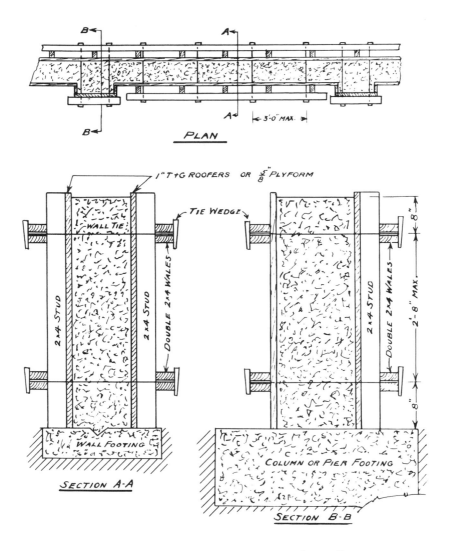

Fig. 23 Wall forms—low grade bearing walls.

form also has a metal circular column head, to help distribute the floor slab load evenly over the column.

If poured before the floor, column forms must be braced to the ground on all four sides, to keep them from moving or tipping while being filled and vibrated. Figures 24–29 show column forms.

8.   Beam and Girder Forms

Generally, the beam and girder forms are made up in the form yard. They are placed on top of the shores by crane or by hand-operated derrick. The bottom of a beam or girder form is made either of one or two pieces of 2 in. dressed lumber (depending on the width of the beam or girder), or ¾ in. plywood. If the concrete is to be exposed, the sides are made of ⅝ in. plywood boards. If the concrete will be covered with plaster or other material, square edge boards can be used.

For beams or girders over 18 in. deep, one or two rows of metal wall ties can be used to keep the form from spreading while the concrete is being placed. Double 2 x 4 walers, as used on walls, should be used to hold each row of ties. Near the top of the beam or girder forms, 1 x 4 or 1 x 6 rough square edge boards should be nailed to both side beam or girder forms, with the wide side against the form, to support the 3 x 4 or 4 x 4 wood form floor joists. To stiffen the beam and girder form sides, 1¼ x 4 or 2 x 4 wood battens are nailed vertically to the beam or girder sides, from top to bottom of the form. The walers and rough 1 x 4 or 1 x 6 boards to carry the wood form floor joists are nailed to these battens.

For shallow beams and girders, the sides and bottom of the form can be ⅝ in. plywood. The bottom of the beam form can rest on two 3 x 4s, one on each edge of the beam or girder; 1¼ x 4 battens, 16 in. on centers, are placed vertically on both side forms. The battens are flush with the bottom of the 3 x 4s that support the bottom of the beam form. The beam or girder form sits on top of 4 x 4 wood shores with a 4 x 4 "T" head nailed to the top of the shore, at right angles to it. A 1 x 4 wood kicker is nailed against the 1¼ x 4 battens, with the 4 in. dimension resting on the "T" heads of the shore. Do this on both sides of the form. The "T" head consists of a piece of 4 x 4 wide enough to take the beam form and the 1 x 4 kickers on both sides of the beam. The 4 x 4 "T" is nailed to the top of the 4 x 4 or 4 x 6 shore with a wood cleat. Near the top of the

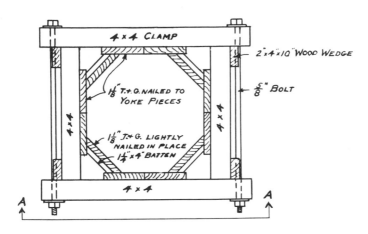

SECTION THROUGH FORM

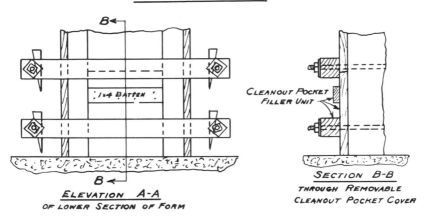

ELEVATION A-A
OF LOWER SECTION OF FORM

SECTION B-B
THROUGH REMOVABLE
CLEANOUT POCKET COVER

DETAIL OF CLEANOUT POCKET

Fig. 24 Column forms—octagonal, wood.

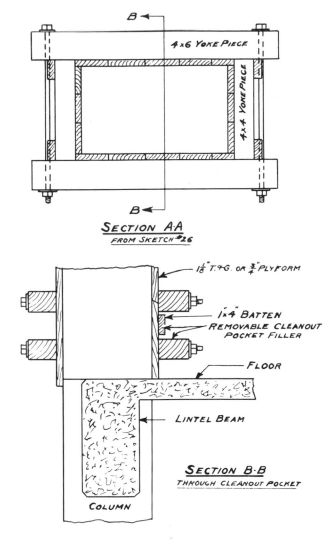

B ←

4 x 6 Yoke Piece

4 x 4 Yoke Piece

B ←

SECTION A·A
FROM SKETCH #26

1⅛" T.⅌G. OR ¾" PLYFORM

1×4" BATTEN
REMOVABLE CLEANOUT
POCKET FILLER

FLOOR

LINTEL BEAM

SECTION B·B
THROUGH CLEANOUT POCKET

COLUMN

Fig. 25 Column forms—exterior details.

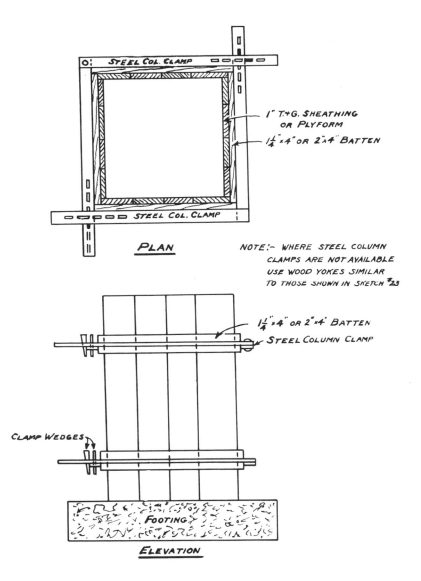

Fig. 26   Pier and pedestal forms—wood and steel clamps.

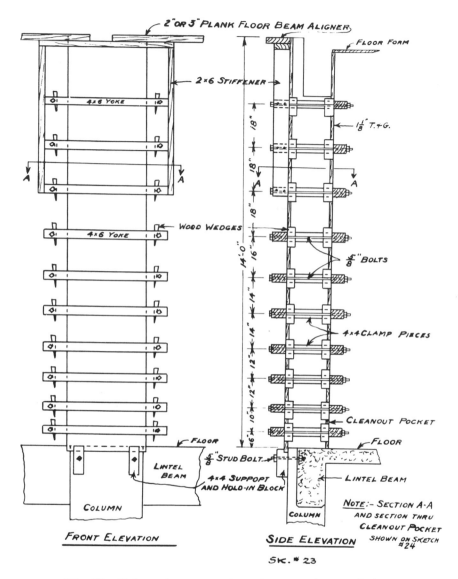

Fig. 27 Column forms—exterior columns—using wood clamps.

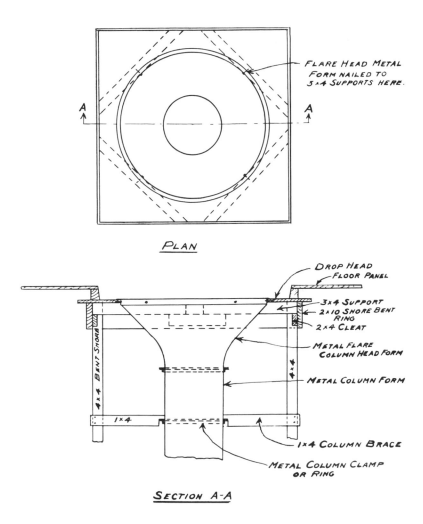

PLAN

FLARE HEAD METAL
FORM NAILED TO
3×4 SUPPORTS HERE.

DROP HEAD
FLOOR PANEL

3×4 SUPPORT
2×10 SHORE BENT
RING
2×4 CLEAT

METAL FLARE
COLUMN HEAD FORM

METAL COLUMN FORM

4×4 BENT SHORE

4×4

1×4

1×4 COLUMN BRACE

METAL COLUMN CLAMP
OR RING

SECTION A-A

Fig. 28   Column forms—round, metal.

59

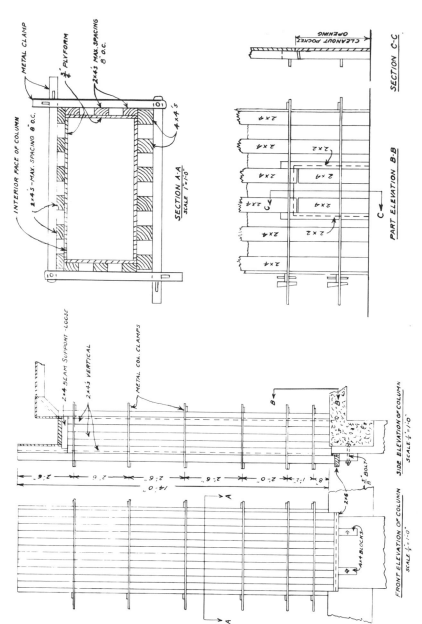

Fig. 29 Column forms—alternate exterior column forms for use with flat slab forms.

beam form is nailed a 2 x 4 ribbon strip that carries the 3 x 4 floor form joists or spreaders. The tops of the 1¼ x 4 battens are cut off 1¼ in. below the top of the plywood form sides, to take a 1¼ x 1¼ in. continuous wood strip that holds the beam form sides in alignment. Some beam and girder forms are illustrated in Figs. 30–32.

9. Shores and Reshores

Shores to carry deep beams and girders should consist of 2 4 x 4s with a cleat nailed to the top to keep them in position. Shores for both deep and shallow beams are placed on top of the 3 or 4 in. thick mud sills with two wood wedges between the bottom of the shore and the mud sill. Patented adjustable shores may be rented or purchased as alternatives. These shores can be adjusted for various heights.

On all wood floor forms, 6 x 6 wood reshores are placed both under the middle of the bay and halfway between the columns. The plywood slab form against which a reshore is placed is cut out around and close to the reshores. The reshores are left in place and not disturbed while the floor form is being stripped. Fresh concrete is weak in compression, and the reshores keep the floor from cracking. The floor forms should be left in place 6 or 7 days. The reshores are left in place 28 days, or until the concrete achieves its full design strength (if one or two floors above the reshored floor have been placed). The shores carrying the floor above exert a heavy temporary load on the new reshored floor.

10. Floor Forms and Floor Reinforcing Rods

The first step in building floor forms is to set up the column forms. The columns can be concreted either before the floor forms are started or after they have been built. For this discussion we assume that the columns will be placed a few days before the floor.

Prior to setting column forms, the ground under the floor that is to be formed and poured is leveled off to the bottom of the gravel or crushed stone fill under the basement slab. The gravel or crushed stone (whichever is specified) is then placed onto the ground and rolled, if possible, for compaction. The column forms are set up and braced, and mud sills

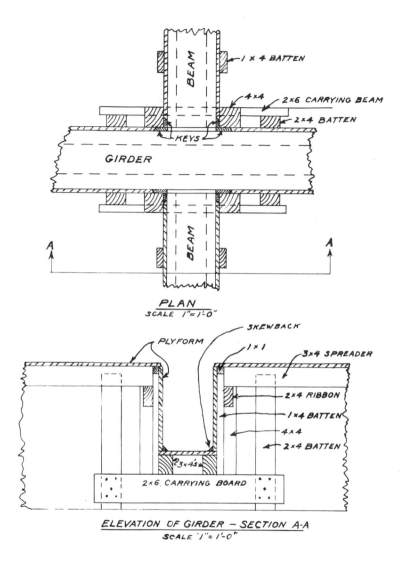

Fig. 30 Floor forms—detail of beam and girder intersection.

62

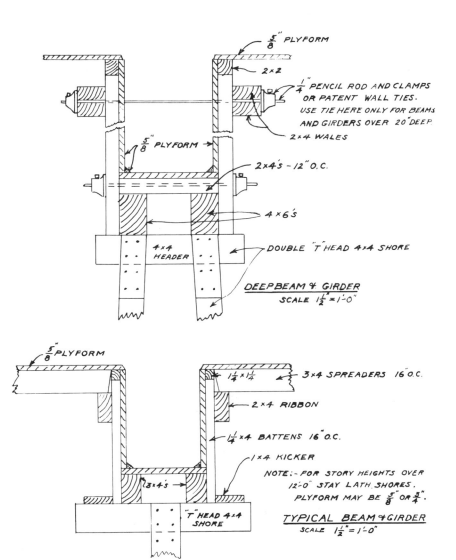

Fig. 31 Floor forms—beam and girder details.

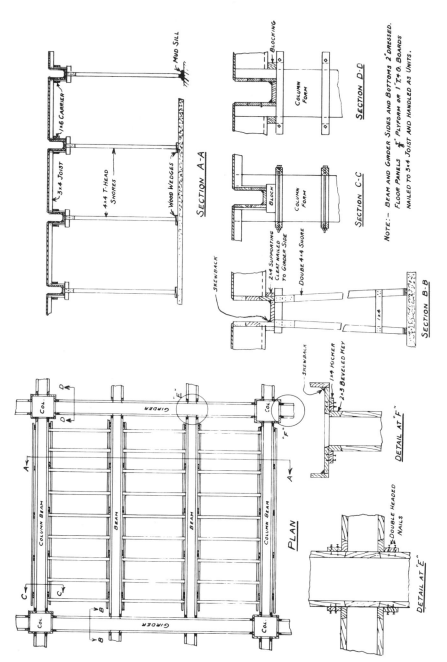

Fig. 32 Floor forms—typical beam and girder.

are placed on the crushed stone or gravel fill. The mud sills are placed where the shores and reshores are to be installed (generally about 3½ to 4 ft apart), with additional mud sills under the beam and girder locations.

Mud sills are generally used lumber, either 3 x 6s, 3 x 8s, 3 x 10s, or 3 x 12s. The shores are generally 4 x 4 wood shores, or the patent adjustable variety. These shores are spaced about 5 ft apart on top of the mud sills, with two wood wedges placed between the mud sill and the shore. Next 1 x 4 wood cleats are nailed on two opposite sides of the 4 x 4 shores, extending above the shores about 6 in., and 4 x 6 wood stringers with the 6 in. side vertical are dropped on top of the 4 x 4 shores and nailed to the 1 x 4 wood cleats. Adjustable patented shores have a special head piece that takes these 4 x 6 stringers.

Floor spreaders, which are either 3 x 4s or 4 x 4s, carry the plywood on which the slab is placed; these are laid loosely on top of the 4 x 6 stringers, about 12 or 14 in. apart. Where these 3 x 4 wood spreaders butt against the floor beam and girder forms, a 2 x 4 ribbon strip with the 4 in. dimension vertical is nailed to the face of the batten carries the ends of the spreaders. If the columns are to be placed along with the floor, these spreaders rest on wood cleats nailed to the sides of the column forms. Standard ⅝ or ¾ in. 4 x 8 plywood sheets, previously dipped in form oil, are laid on top of the floor spreaders and tacked down with a few short nails to keep them from blowing away.

Flat slab floors are now being used to a greater extent than previously. For these floors the column form is placed last, but the flared metal column head form is placed first. To receive this flared head, a square scaffold is built consisting of four 4 x 4 wood legs. The center of the column is first established, and the scaffold is placed by centering it on the column center. The scaffold, which is square and large enough to take the drop head panel, is placed on the mud sills, with two wood wedges between the mud sill and the four 4 x 4 carrying posts. For support, 2 x 10s are nailed near the top of the four posts at an elevation required to take the drop head panel. A 2 x 4 cleat is nailed near the bottom of the column side of the 2 x 10. The four 3 x 4 spreaders are placed diagonally between the centers of the column bents. These 3 x 4s support the slab forms for the drop head, which can be ⅝ in. plywood, or 1 x 6 tongue and groove boards. If the bottom of the drop head is to be covered by plaster, the drop head floor is made large enough to take the square four-sided drop panel around the column.

Next the drop panel is then cut out to take the round, flared head, metal column form. The flared head metal column form is nailed to the 3 x 4 spreaders and a beveled piece of 3 x 4 is nailed to the drop head panel, to take the flat slab panel. For easier stripping, 2 x 8 column bent spacers are nailed into the column bents, or scaffold, to keep them in line and to support the 4 x 6 stringers for the floor slab.

After the vertical column reinforcing bars have been installed, the metal column form is installed, and 1 x 4 wood column braces are nailed to the 4 x 4 scaffold posts horizontally and pressed against the metal column clamps. These hold the sections of the metal column form in position, to help keep the column from shifting while being placed.

Next to be placed in position are 4 x 4 shores, spaced about 5 ft in one direction at the mud sills and 3 ft 6 in. or 4 ft 9 in. at right angles; these shores carry the 4 x 6 wood stringers. The shores rest on two wood wedges laid either on top of the mud sills, or on the floor below, in the case of an upper floor. On top of the 4 x 6 stringers, 3 x 4 spreaders are laid about 14 in. apart. Then ⅝ or ¾ in. plywood is placed on top of the 3 x 4 spreaders and tacked down lightly.

Electric light ceiling boxes are then nailed to the floor slab plywood form, in the location of the ceiling lights below. Metal sleeves for all pipework that penetrates the floor slab are nailed to the plywood and filled with scrap paper or sand to keep the sleeve from filling up with concrete.

Anchor slots for brick anchors (to tie the brickwork into the structural building forms) are nailed to the exterior fall of the spandrel beam forms. When all sleeves, boxes, and other elements that are to be built into the floor slab, are in place, reinforcing steel accessories, such as high chairs, slab spacers, and beam and girder bolsters are nailed to the floor at the required places to carry the reinforcing steel. The bottom layer of reinforcing steel rods is then placed. As soon as this has been done, conduit is run to connect ceiling light receptacle boxes, which were nailed to the slab forms, and the installation of electric light switches near door openings, outlet receptacles, and other electrical equipment can proceed. Take extreme care to install conduit turnups so that they fall inside the partitions and are not turned up in door openings. The line and grade crew should lay out both sides of all partitions as soon as the floor slab form is installed. This permits the mechanical trades to install their sleeves, conduit turnups, and so on, in the proper places. It costs a great deal to correct locations after the floor slab has been placed. Flat slab floor forms are illustrated in Figs. 33–38.

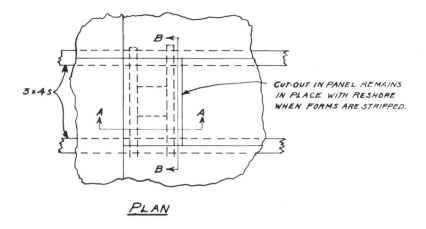

3 x 4 S

CUT-OUT IN PANEL REMAINS
IN PLACE WITH RESHORE
WHEN FORMS ARE STRIPPED.

PLAN

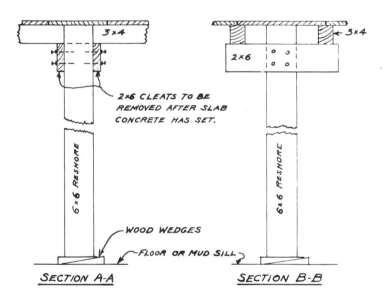

3 x 4

2×6 CLEATS TO BE
REMOVED AFTER SLAB
CONCRETE HAS SET.

6×6 RESHORE

WOOD WEDGES

FLOOR OR MUD SILL

SECTION A-A

3×4

2×6

6×6 RESHORE

SECTION B-B

NOTE :- RESHORE IS SET INTO POSITION BEFORE SLAB IS CONCRETED.

Fig. 33 Floor forms—flat slab, reshore details.

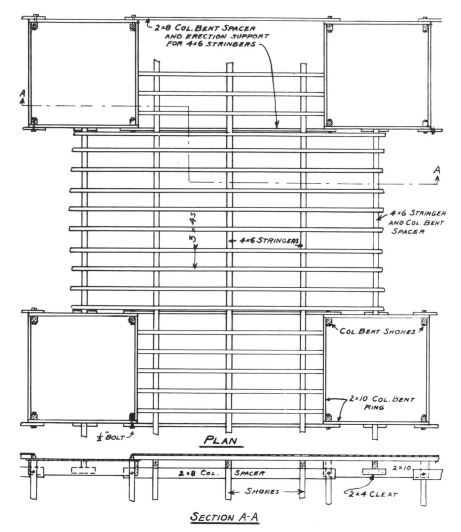

Fig. 34 Floor forms—flat slab using column bents, erection details.

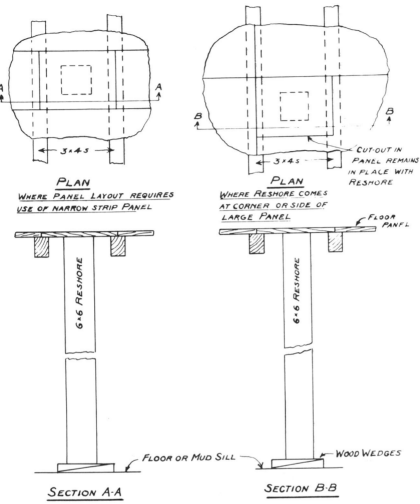

PLAN

WHERE PANEL LAYOUT REQUIRES
USE OF NARROW STRIP PANEL

PLAN

WHERE RESHORE COMES
AT CORNER OR SIDE OF
LARGE PANEL

CUT-OUT IN
PANEL REMAINS
IN PLACE WITH
RESHORE

← 3×4S →

FLOOR
PANEL

6×6 RESHORE

6×6 RESHORE

FLOOR OR MUD SILL

WOOD WEDGES

SECTION A-A

SECTION B-B

NOTE: — RESHORES ARE SET AND WEDGED IN PLACE AFTER CONCRETE
IS SET AND BEFORE STRIPPING OF FLOOR FORMS IS STARTED.
AVOID DRIVING SHORE WEDGES WITH HEAVY HAMMERS.

Fig. 35 Floor forms—flat slab, reshore details.

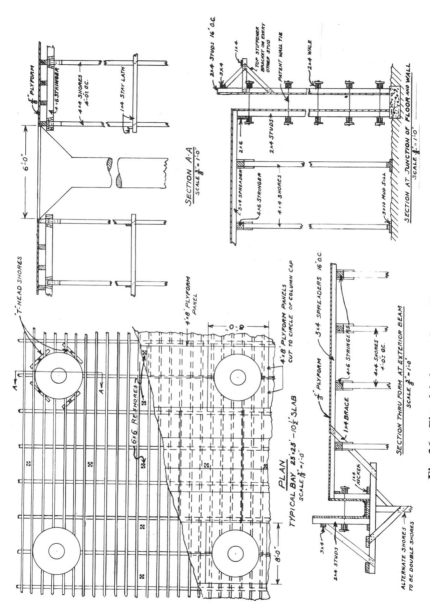

Fig. 36 Flat slab forms—flat ceiling, no drop heads at columns.

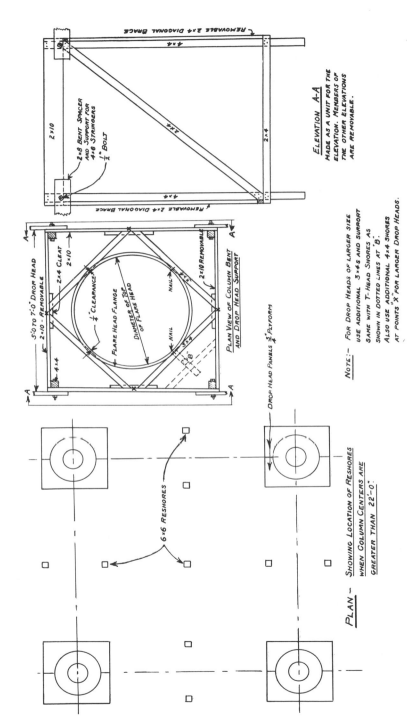

Fig. 37 Floor forms—flat slab details showing reshoring for bays over 22 ft square and column bent details.

71

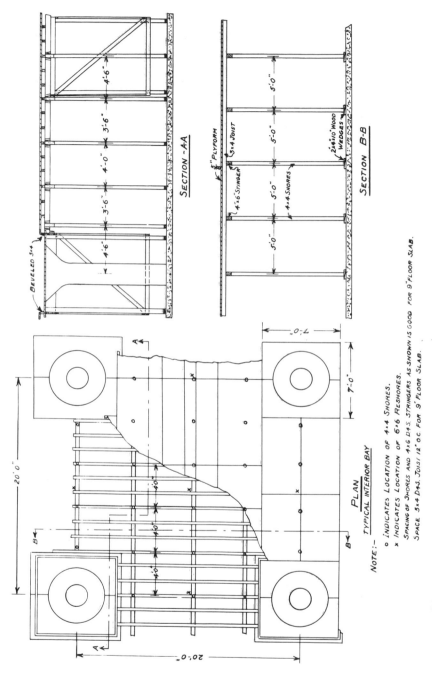

SECTION - AA

BEVELED 3×4

4'-6" 3'-6" 4'-0" 3'-6" 4'-6"

SECTION B-B

3"PLYFORM

4'×6"STRINGER

3×4 JOIST

2"×10"WOOD WEDGES

4×4 SHORES

5'-0" 5'-0" 5'-0" 5'-0"

20'-0"

PLAN
TYPICAL INTERIOR BAY

20'-0"

7'-0"

7'-0"

4'-0" 4'-0" 4'-0"

NOTE:-

o INDICATES LOCATION OF 4×4 SHORES.
x INDICATES LOCATION OF 6×6 RESHORES.
SPACING OF SHORES AND 4×6 D4S STRINGERS AS SHOWN IS GOOD FOR 9"FLOOR SLAB.
SPACE 3×4 D4S JOIST 12"OC FOR 9"FLOOR SLAB.

Fig. 38 Floor forms—flat slab, bays up to 22 ft square showing use of column bents for drop heads.

11. *Placing Floor Concrete*

Use of Crane, Concrete Hand Buggies, Gasoline-Driven
Concrete Buggies, and Concrete Pumps

Concrete contractors differ in their methods of placing floors. Some use a crane, carrying a one cubic yard concrete bottom drop bucket, to lift the concrete from the ready-mix trucks to the floor in work. In one method the crane dumps the concrete directly on top of the floor forms. Another method is to set up a 2 or 3 cubic yard metal concrete hopper directly on the floor forms, with additional wood shores under the hopper. The concrete is dumped by the crane from the concrete bucket into the hopper. Then the fresh concrete is wheeled to its dump position on the floor in rubber-tired buggies (Figs. 39 and 40).

The buggies go on concrete run panels, placed on top of wooden horses, which are built about 14 in. high and about 6 in. wider than the concrete run panels. Two tapered 4 x 4s form the legs, with two 1 x 4s or 1 x 6s

Fig. 39 Pouring concrete by crane from truck into a hopper on the roof, then wheeling the concrete into position. Restricted area prevented the use of large crane to place concrete directly into the forms. Today a tower crane could have been used.

Fig. 40 Concrete truck backed up to the side of the building, pouring directly into forms.

nailed to the top of the 4 x 4 legs to tie them together. The leg bottoms are tapered to make it easier to remove the legs from the fresh concrete.

Sometimes "scootcretes" or their equivalent are used to carry the concrete. The "power buggy" has a small gasoline engine to propel the small hopper-shaped body that carries the concrete. The hopper is mounted in front of the driver-operator, who dumps his load of concrete by moving a drop lever. If power buggies are used, the concrete run panels must be made wider and stronger to take the additional live load. Also the concrete horses that support the run panels must be strengthened. The power buggy carries more fresh mix than a hand-pushed concrete buggy, and works faster.

The operators must be careful not to run off the run panels. For both power and hand-pushed concrete buggies there must be bypasses set up, allowing units to pass each other. This is done by placing two parallel run panel sets on horses beside the runways at reasonable intervals, depending on the amount of traffic.

Using Hoist Towers

Some contractors prefer setting up a concrete hoist tower. If the building covers a large area, two towers are set up. Since a tower must be built after the structural concrete has been placed to lift material for brickwork, interior partitions, all materials, and small equipment that go into the construction, why not build the towers first and use them to hoist the structural concrete? The tower can be constructed of metal pipe or of wood.

The legs of a wood tower are made of 4 x 6s, with 2 x 6 horizontals on each of the four sides, spaced about 4 ft apart. To keep the tower from racking or twisting, 2 x 6 cross bracing, one brace to each side of the tower, is installed between the horizontal 2 x 6 braces. The tower should be double, containing a 1 cubic yard concrete bucket in one half, and a platform lift in the other. This is for hoisting masonry and other building construction materials.

A "Chicago boom," for lifting reinforcing steel and other items from the ground to the various floors, is secured to one of the tower legs away from the building. This boom is built of wood or metal and is long enough to reach the top floor. The boom has a ⅝ or ¾ in. diameter wire rope cable, carrying a hook. The cable passes over sheave blocks on both ends of the boom. Then it passes through a snatch block connected to the bottom of the tower leg, to the drum of the hoisting engine. The other end of the cable is tied to a large hook used to pick up the load.

Wire rope cable slings are made up with a hook attached to each end. A small hoop in the middle of each sling takes the hoisting cable. These slings are wrapped around bundles of reinforcing steel bars, electric conduit, and so on, for raising.

One end of the Chicago boom (Fig. 41) is secured to the tower leg by means of a swivel block. The other end extends at an angle of about 45° from the tower leg, above the swivel block; tag lines (manila rope), controlled from the ground, guide the load on the Chicago boom to the proper floor. The other tag line is used from the floor itself to pull the load into the floor.

A three-drum gasoline-driven hoist engine is used to operate the moving parts of the tower. One drum controls the concrete bucket, the second controls the hoist platform, and the third operates the Chicago boom.

A bell is mounted in the shed that houses the engine and its operator.

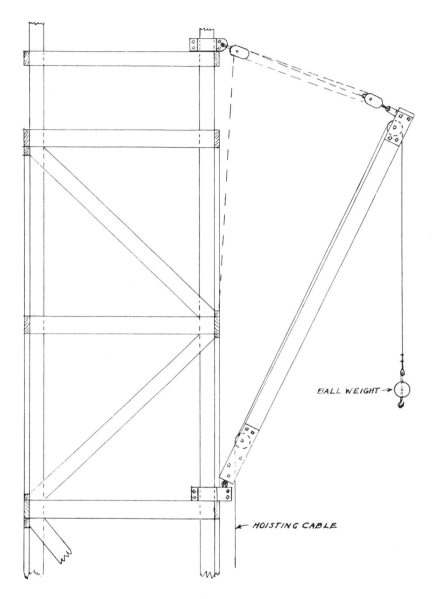

BALL WEIGHT →

← HOISTING CABLE

Fig. 41 Chicago boom for hoisting.

A clothesline attached to the bell is secured to one leg of the tower, so that the bell can be rung from any floor. Build a platform to connect each floor to the tower.

The hoist tower appears to be more adaptable than the crane. The crane has only one hook, whereas the tower has the equivalent of three. After the concrete has been placed each day, the tower can be used to hoist other items the crane cannot handle.

Other Types of Crane

Other crane types in use include tower cranes mounted on a truck or on a wide-gauged railroad track. Climbing cranes, set up inside the building itself, are raised as the upper floors rise.

The common truck crane is also widely used. However very tall cranes may be hazardous because they sometimes tip over; also, an exceptionally long boom may fail under heavy loads. There have been many recorded accidents with very tall truck cranes. (The rig itself must be set on a level hardwood beam platform. Counterweights and outriggers have to be balanced and leveled from proper moment calculations. Maximum practical truck-crane boom height is about 20 stories).

12. Stripping Floor Forms

After the concrete floor has been placed and cured for about 7 days, column and floor forms are ready to be stripped. These forms are leap-frogged to the floor just placed. Always be sure that there are sufficient reshores left in place. If the weather is cool, it might prove safe to install additional 4 x 4 shapes to take the load of the new floor forms being erected, above the slab that is being stripped. Floor form stripping is done by specially trained stripping crews, using crowbars, long hooked bars, and other tools especially designed for stripping. In some localities unions may insist that carpenters help with the stripping.

One or two bays are stripped at a time, to lessen the danger of floor cracking. First the shores are removed and leapfrogged to the next floor above (by the Chicago boom or by crane, or passed up by hand). The 4 x 6 stringers and the 3 x 4 spreaders are lowered to the floor (by using hooks attached to long handles), then raised to the floor above. Sometimes the plywood sticks to the concrete and has to be worked loose with stripping hooks.

Exposed concrete is pointed after the column and floor forms have been removed and raised to the floor just stripped. Cement masons, working on rolling scaffolds, patch up the "honeycombs" and grind off the mortar that has collected between the plywood joints.

If the concrete is to be painted, it must be left as smooth as possible, so that any deficiencies in the finished surface will not show through the paint. If the concrete is to be covered with plaster or other material, the concrete painting job does not have to be perfect. A minimal standard of workmanship is expected: just fill up the "honeycomb," smooth it over, and remove the larger joint rise.

13. *Placing Concrete Walls for Basements*

The concrete for basement walls is generally placed by chuting it direct from the ready-mix trucks into the wall forms through metal or wood chutes. This is not good practice. Sometimes the workmen become careless and let the wet concrete pile up too high in the wall form, which tends to segregate the coarse aggregate from the mortar. It also puts too much spot pressure on the wall form.

It is better and safer practice to build a scaffold alongside the wall at its top. A concrete hopper is set up on the scaffold, and the concrete flows into the hopper, down a chute from the ready-mix trucks. Concrete is then wheeled to the wall form from the hopper in rubber-tired concrete buggies. Though more expensive, this method results in more even distribution of the concrete, eliminates cold joints and segregation, and puts no additional pressure on the wall forms.

After the wall has been placed, a beveled 2 x 4 or 3 x 4 should be inserted parallel to it, centered on top of the concrete, to form a keyway, either for the floor slab concrete that will be placed on top of the wall, or for the next lift of the rising wall.

If the vertical reinforcing bars in the wall rise too short for the proper bond for the concrete to be placed on top of the wall, extra reinforcing bars (bond bars) must be inserted into the concrete on both faces of the wall. These bond bars must extend 40 diameters into the wall concrete and 40 diameters out of the wall for proper bond.

14. Reinforcing Steel: Basic Design

The design of the reinforcing steel is the function of the structural engineer. His drawings, schedules, and specifications must give the job staff enough information to fabricate and place the steel rods in the proper positions. If the information is insufficient, the job engineer and the job superintendent should meet with the structural engineer to discuss the deficiences. The job staff should never guess or rely on its judgment to fill in the missing information. Adherence to the following practices generally is required by building codes:

1. Reinforcing rods must be free of loose mill scale.
2. Reinforcing rods must be free of oil or grease coatings.
3. Reinforcing rods must be free of minor or major bends, *other* than those shown on the Bending Schedule.
4. The clearance between straight bars should not be less than 1½ times the diameter of the round bars, or 2 times the diameter of the straight bars.
5. The spacing between bars should not be less than 1 in., or less than 1⅓ times the maximum size of the coarse aggregate in the concrete.
6. Splices in bars must be made at the points of minimum stress or at the point of inflection.

Reinforcing rods should not be placed too close to the exterior faces of concrete surfaces that will be exposed either to weather or to the soil. Reinforcing rods in footings and foundations should be placed 3 in. from the exposed surfaces or concrete. For concrete floors placed directly on earth, the reinforcing rods should be placed not closer than 2 in. from the lower concrete surface.

Column (vertical) bars should be kept 2 in. away from the column form face. To maintain this distance, prefabricated cement and sand mortar "doughnuts" are placed over the vertical column bars to keep them away from the form. These "doughnuts" are 6 in. outside diameter and 2 in. thick, with a hole in the center tapering from 2 to 2½ in.

"Chairs" and beam bolsters hold in place the bottom steel for beams and girders. Stirrups must be kept away from the sides of beams and girders because if they are too close, the rusting of the stirrups will spall the concrete surface. This becomes quite noticeable after a time, thus must be avoided. The "doughnut" can be used to prevent such spalling.

15. *Proper Placing of Reinforcing Steel for Concrete Work*

The duty of the job field force is to be sure the reinforcing steel bars are placed in and on the form (as required by the structural drawings and specifications) before the concrete is placed. Improper placing of reinforcing rods can negate good design and even cause building failure. Only assistant superintendents with experience and a desire to do the job right should be given this responsibility. Improper placing of reinforcing steel cannot be tolerated.

With assurance that reinforcing steel will be properly placed, designers can specify structural members of small cross-sectional area that are still strong enough to carry the design loads. Concrete and reinforcing rods expand and contract with temperature changes at about the same rate. This makes it possible to combine these different building materials. For more information on combinations, see *Composite Construction Methods,* by J. P. Cook, P. E. (Wiley, 1977).

To make identification simpler, a numbering system has been devised for reinforcing steel bar sizes. These numbers are rolled into the bars to eliminate mistakes. The cross-reference table below gives the sizes and numbers.

Size (in.)	Numbers
¼ round	#2
⅜ round	#3
½ round	#4
⅝ round	#5
¾ round	#6
⅞ round	#7
1 round	#8
1⅛ round	#9
1¼ round	#10
1⅜ round	#11

Generally, representatives for the architects or structural engineers check the size, spacing, and location of the reinforcing steel rods after

Fig. 42 The engineer's inspector checking the reinforcing before the concrete pour.

they have been situated and before the concrete is placed (Fig. 42). If this inspection is not made, the job superintendent should assign an assistant superintendent who is thoroughly familiar with the placing of reinforcing steel rods to make this inspection, before every concrete placement.

The order for supplying reinforcing rods is made up by the purchasing department. It should give a schedule for the delivery of the steel from the mill. Rods arrive by trailer trucks, railroad cars, and ship. The staff orders bar shipments as required by the job.

The reinforcing rods should be ground stored on top of timbers, to prevent rusting and for greater ease in picking them up. The storage area must be big enough to provide place for storing rods according to bar sizes and lengths. You also need room for bent or straight steel rods that have been fabricated and are ready to be placed in the building. Reinforcing rods for each floor, walls, columns, and footings, should be stored separately and marked. In winter rods must be covered to prevent snow and ice from damaging the steel.

Reinforcing rods can be cut to length and shape in the mill, then shipped to the job. However most local unions require the rods to be cut and bent to the required shape on the site. Bending on the job may be done by using power bending machines or by using bending blocks nailed to the bending bench. The rods are put in the bending blocks at the required bending places, as shown on the drawings or tags (Fig. 44), then bent by hand, using long or short hollow pipes for leverage. Figures 45–48 illustrate various types of bending.

16.   *Reinforcing Steel Classifications*

Footing steel is usually made of straight rods hooked at each end, and formed into a mat with bars about 3 in. apart in both directions (or as sepcified on the drawings). The hooks are placed on the bars, and the mats are made up on a flat wood bench, then placed inside the footing form on pieces of brick or concrete blocks. These keep the rods about 3 in. above the ground. The edges of the mat are kept back from the outside face of the footing about 3 in. on all sides. Bond bars to the concrete column above are inserted in the center of the footing after it has been placed. If the footing is to carry a steel column, anchor bolts are placed in a wood template nailed to the top of the footing form before the concrete is placed.

Column steel consists of straight bars placed vertically, with light steel hoops tied around all bars at specified distances. If the column above is to be smaller in section than the lower portion of the column, the straight bars are bent below the floor the column carries. This keeps the bars that are to be buried in the column above inside the upper portion of the column. This bending is done on the bench before the bars are placed in the form. To ensure that the column steel is in the proper position to fit inside the column above, 2 x 4s with tapered ends are placed between the lower column steel and the column form.

The concrete column steel sometimes is made up on two carpenter's horses, about 4 ft high, then dropped into the column form, or set up before the form is applied. Sometimes the column steel is assembled in place, and the column form built around it.

Wall steel consists of vertical straight bars, to which horizontal straight bars are tied. (The sizes and spacing of both types of bar are given in the specifications.) Wall steel may be specified for one side of a wall, both sides of a wall, or both sides and in the middle, if the wall is comparatively wide, or if the forces acting on the wall demand this additional reinforcement.

If a wall is to be placed directly above a lower wall to be poured, the vertical bars in the lower wall should protrude 25 bar diameters above the top of the lower wall for proper bending, between the two walls.

If a wall is only one story, the vertical straight bars should be bent at right angles to the wall at the top of the wall, so that the rods can be buried into the concrete floor slab above, thus tying the wall and floor slab together. Care must be taken to ensure that the rods are bent at the proper elevation to receive the floor slab.

17. Floor and Roof Steel

It is very important that the reinforcing steel for floors and roofs be spotted in the exact location shown in the structural drawings as the floors and the roof concrete are being placed. The correct position of the reinforcing rods must be maintained; otherwise the steel will lose its effectiveness in both compression and tension. Failures may result, particularly for cantilever slabs.

Workmen can walk on wood ramps to carry steel rods to higher or lower levels. Figure 43 illustrates that pouring concrete is not a one-trade operation.

18. Footing Steel

The placing of footing reinforcing steel rods can be done either by making up the reinforcing steel mats outside the footing, or by assembling the steel mat in place. Take extreme care when building the mat in place, particularly if the soil is bad. If the soil under the footing is low bearing, it is safer to hang the reinforcing steel mat from timbers or heavy steel rods supported on opposite sides of the footing form. Use #8 or #10 soft annealed wire to hang the mat. For floor slabs with top and bottom layers of reinforcing steel rods to be placed directly on low bearing soil, make special provisions to support the reinforcing steel. The accessories

Fig. 43   Wire mesh and reinforcing ready for pour. Note insert for pipes and conduits, stub ups, and splice boxes in position.

to be used should be placed on parts of brick, small prefabricated concrete slabs 2 or 3 in. thick, or on any other practical material.

Rod men must be careful in assembling the mat by poor soil. If the soil is soft, it would be safer to assemble the mat outside the footing, then hang it from supports, as previously described.

19.   *Wall Steel and Pouring Wall*

Wall reinforcement is placed after one side of the wall form has been set up. Curtain and parapet walls are formed on the outside first, permitting the rod men to work on the floor or on the roof. When one side form of the wall is in position, the position of the vertical and horizontal bars is marked on the form with colored crayon or keel. The vertical rods are then set up and tied to nails driven into the wall form. If the wall is very high, a steel rod can be nailed horizontally to the form near the top of the wall, and the vertical rods are tied to this horizontal rod. The horizontal wall steel is then placed into position. If the wall has reinforcing rods on both faces, the rods at the other wall form are placed into position at the required distance from the form, which already has been set up. This distance is maintained by spreaders nailed to the form in place. The missing wall form is then erected and tied to the first wall form by wall ties.

When concrete vibrators are used to help place concrete into the wall forms, the vibrator must be kept away from the reinforcing rods. If the vibrator strikes a rod, the ties holding the reinforcing in place may break, and the rest of the steel rods may be forced out of position. If this happens, it is very difficult to put the rods back into correct position.

Construction joints have to be placed in walls and floors if either component is too large to be poured in one working day. If the steel rods do not run through the construction joints, bond bars must be placed 40 diameters on both sides of the joint to tie the two placements together. Construction joints in the walls, floors, beams, and girders, must be made in the center third of the cross-sectional area.

Prior to pouring the concrete, the reinforcing steel must be checked by the assistant superintendent in charge of positioning reinforcing steel. Use the placing drawings and the reinforcing steel schedule to answer the following items:

1. Are all the rods the proper size?
2. Is the proper number of rods (both straight and bent) included in the layout?
3. Are the bends properly placed?
4. Are the bars uniformly spaced and at the specified distance apart?
5. Are the laps in the bars in accordance with the specifications?
6. Are there enough reinforcing steel accessories, and are they properly positioned?
7. Are all steel rods properly tied together?

The steel reinforcing rods should be checked after the mechanical trades have completed their work, and again during concrete placing, since both these operations tend to disturb the position of the steel rods. A rod man with good experience in steel rod placing should make these checks.

If steel is placed in winter time, it should be covered with canvas overnight to keep off snow and ice. Figures 44–48 show how to handle rein-

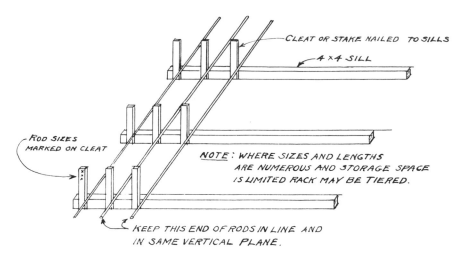

CLEAT OR STAKE NAILED TO SILLS

4 X 4 SILL

ROD SIZES
MARKED ON CLEAT

NOTE: WHERE SIZES AND LENGTHS
ARE NUMEROUS AND STORAGE SPACE
IS LIMITED RACK MAY BE TIERED.

KEEP THIS END OF RODS IN LINE AND
IN SAME VERTICAL PLANE.

STEEL STORAGE RACK

SKETCH NO. 1

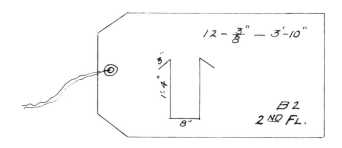

$12 - \frac{3}{8}" - 3'-10"$

3"

1'-4"

8"

B 2
2 $\underline{ND}$ FL.

STIRRUP AND COLUMN HOOP
IDENTIFICATION TAG

SKETCH NO. 2

Fig. 44   Storage rack and identification tag.

86

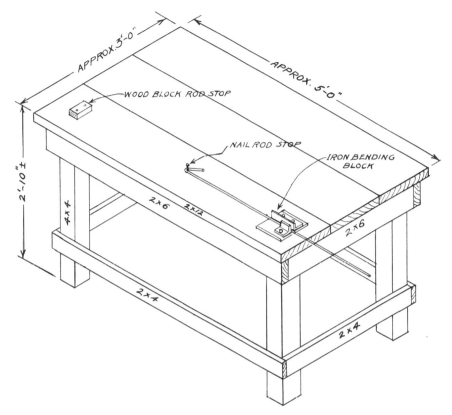

Fig. 45 Bending block and bench for light bending.

forcing steel rods when a power bender is not available, and typical placements.

20. *Miscellaneous Items Relating to Forms, Reinforcing Steel, and Concrete Work*

Use of Polyethylene Films

Polyethylene is used for vapor seals, protection of materials, curing of
concrete, and dampproofing. It is also very useful for placing on top of
the gravel or crushed stone base under concrete slabs on the ground. This
material keeps moisture out of the concrete slab and keeps the sand and

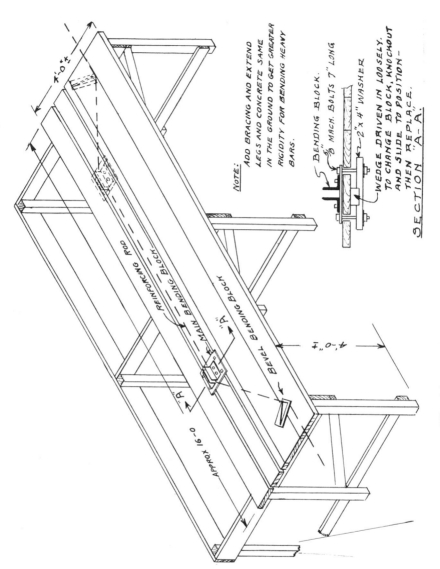

Fig. 46 Bending block and bench for heavy bending.

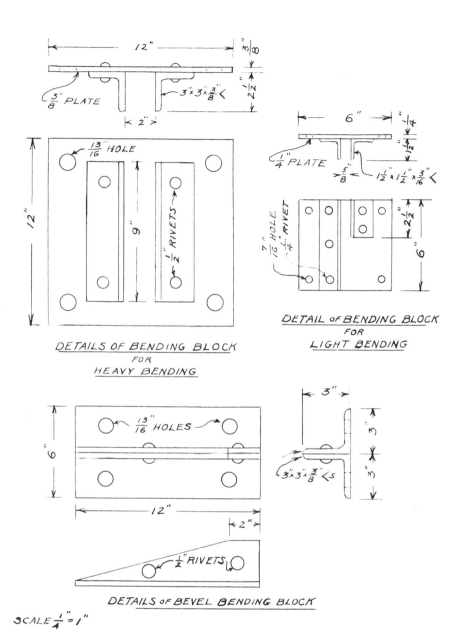

Fig. 47 Bending block.

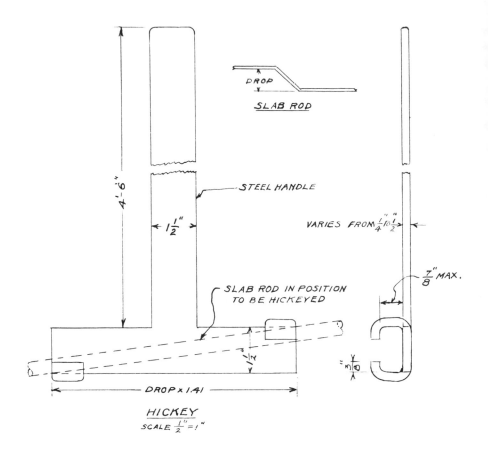

DROP

SLAB ROD

STEEL HANDLE

$1\frac{1}{2}''$

VARIES FROM $\frac{1}{4}''$ to $\frac{1}{2}''$

$4'\text{-}6''$

$\frac{7}{8}''$ MAX.

SLAB ROD IN POSITION
TO BE HICKEYED

$1\frac{1}{2}''$

$\frac{3}{8}''$

DROP x 1.41

HICKEY
SCALE $\frac{1''}{2} = 1''$

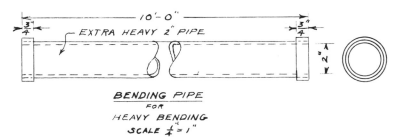

$10'\text{-}0''$

$\frac{3}{4}''$

EXTRA HEAVY 2" PIPE

$\frac{3}{4}''$

$2''$

BENDING PIPE
FOR
HEAVY BENDING
SCALE $\frac{1''}{4} = 1''$

Fig. 48 Steel hickey and bending pipe.

90

cement paste in the concrete from seeping into the ground. All these components must remain in the concrete.

Polyethylene is also used to make dustproof partitions and to cover lumber, forms, marble, granite, reinforcing steel rods, sand, gravel, brick, tile, and other construction materials that must be stored in the open for long times.

Plywood Form Coatings

Some form of treatment must be given the plywood or plyform face that meets the concrete, for the following reasons:

The forms will last longer, and more reuses will be gained from them.

It makes stripping of forms easier, by preventing the wood forms from adhering to the concrete.

It lowers the cost of pointing the concrete after the forms have been removed.

It eliminates the grain marks from the wood on the surface of the concrete, unless these are desired as an architectural feature.

Types of Form Coating

Among the form coatings available today are the following:

1. *Form Oil* (*mop or spray-on*).   This type is not satisfactory because it makes the floor forms slippery; thus it is best to avoid danger by not using this material.

2. *Coated Plywood Forms.*   Form film made by A. C. Horns Company is a quick-drying lacquer. Forms coated with this material can be reused about seven times.

3. *Plywood Kote.*   This trademarked item is similar to form film.

4. *Super Plywood Kote.*   This trademarked material has a rubber base and makes the surface of the plywood harder.

5. *Plastic-Faced Plywood Forms.*   This type of plywood consists of a core of exterior-type fir plywood, coated on each face with a smooth, tough, high-density sheet of cellulose fiber impregnated with phenol-formaldehyde resin. This material is applied under heat and pressure and forms a smooth, dense, hard surface bonded to the plywood. But this type of plywood is somewhat difficult to handle.

6. *Duroform.* This coating is an epoxy resin applied at the mill. Sometimes the plywood panels do not hold up, and breaking and cracking of the corners and edges appear during use.

7. *Hardboard (masonite, etc.).* Hardboard, 3/16 in. thick is used to line ordinary forms. This is an expensive material to use in large quantity.

From these choices, the job superintendent can decide for himself which type of wood form preservative to use.

21. Concrete over Metal Decks

Stone concrete or some types of lightweight aggregate concrete may be used over metal decks. Crushed stone concrete is the best to use. Lightweight aggregates, such as Waylite, Lelite, Haydite, and Gritcrete can be used. If lightweight aggregates are selected, a ¾ in. sand and cement finish should be used, because with lightweight aggregates it is not possible to get a good monolithic finish.

22. Winter Weather Concrete Operations

Concrete operations carried on in winter are exceptionally difficult. Those in charge of concrete work must always be alert to prevent the fresh concrete from freezing. It is also necessary to prevent fires, generally built in salamanders, from burning the winter canvas covers. Actually the form work and the winter weather canvas should be treated with fire-resistant material. Never buy untreated canvas for winter work. Coke salamanders used to prevent the freezing of concrete should always be kept at a safe distance from the canvas and forms. Oil and gas space heaters are more prevalent today. Hay is sometimes used to protect concrete or earth from frost or freezing. If the weather is extremely cold, a canvas cover should be thrown over the hay.

If your job is buying ready-mixed concrete, the concrete batch plans must have facilities for heating the sand, gravel, or crushed stone, while the aggregates are in the bins. If the aggregates are exposed to the weather, they must be covered with canvas or by other means. The plant should also have hot water available. If ready-mix trucks are used, the water tanks on each one must carry hot water. The concrete leaving the ready-mix trucks should be at about 72°F or whatever temperature the structural engineer specifies.

Forms for isolated walls should be prepared before the concrete is poured by placing salt-hay between the 2 x 4 studs on both sides of the wall form. After pouring, the wall should be covered with canvas. Some hay should be placed on top of the wall. This method is used for temperatures that are not extremely cold.

In very cold climates a wood frame should be built over the wall forms with the sides of the framework about 10 ft away from the wall. Put winter weather treated canvases over this framework, on top and enclosing all sides. Electric lights should be placed under this framework. Before the concrete is placed in the wall, coke salamanders or oil-burning space heaters are started outside the enclosure. As soon as the coke in the salamanders has started to burn low, the salamanders are taken inside the framework. Oil-burning heaters are also used extensively. Fire extinguishers and water pails should also be handy inside the framework. If possible, a hose should also be kept inside the framework and connected to the water supply. Build the roof of the framework high enough that it does not catch fire from the heat of the salamanders or sparks from the coke, or from the oil-burning heaters.

Before a structural concrete floor is poured, winter weather canvas should be hung around the perimeter of the space below the floor to enclose it completely. Use canvas to cover about 8 ft above the floor if the weather is extremely cold. Electric lights should be strung over the area to provide good light. Just before the concrete is placed, the coke salamanders or oil-burning heaters should be started outside the enclosure, and when the coke has stopped throwing off sparks, the salamanders should be placed inside the enclosure, under the floor forms. A metal top, such as a mortar pan, should be hung over each salamander or heater to prevent excessive heat from starting fires in the form work above.

Fire extinguishers or water barrels with pails attached should be placed in the enclosure. Again, the best protection is a hose connected to the water supply. Two watchmen (or at least one) should be in the enclosure at all times, to be sure that the canvases are tied down and cannot blow against the salamanders. The salamanders or oil-burning heaters should be kept away from all wood shores and the canvases hung onto the sides. If a salamander has to be close to a wood shore or the enclosing canvas, fireproof protective material should be placed around the salamander. A thermometer must be hung just under the floor forms above, to make sure the forms are not subjected to excessive heat, since the concrete could crack from too much heat. The temperature should be kept in the low 70s.

It is also important the fire watchmen do not drink alcoholic beverages. If they do drink, they may fall asleep, and with no one watching, fires could easily start.

The important aspects of winter weather concrete protection can be summarized as follows:

1. Keep the concrete warm for 5 days before exposing it to the winter temperatures.
2. When the forms are removed, concrete is still weak in compression. Thus while stripping a floor, make sure that the reshores are placed under the floor slab in a properly designed pattern.
3. If the job mixes its own concrete, set up a mixer at the bottom of the hoist tower close enough to permit the mixer to discharge the concrete directly into the concrete bucket that hoists the concrete to the upper floors via the tower. The sand and gravel bins are placed directly behind the mixer. These methods are used to heat the aggregates and water.
4. Heat the sand, gravel, crushed stone, and water with steam. Set up a steam boiler or generator beside the aggregate bins and the mixer. Run steam pipes at the bottom of the bins to allow the steam to work up thru the aggregates to thaw.
5. Use about a 50 hp boiler for large jobs. Steam lines can also be used for removing ice and snow from the stripped floors. Run a steam line up one of the tower legs. Install a valve and water connection for a steam hose at each floor. To remove the snow and ice, connect the steam hose to this riser line.
6. In place of a heatable storage tank, if none is available, place water barrels near the mixer and run a steam line into the barrels to a point just above the bottom. Drawing mixing water from these barrels.
7. Aggregates should contain no frost. They should be kept at around 50°F.
8. Mixing water in the barrels or tank should be heated to above 150°F.

9. The bottoms of exterior columns are very difficult to protect against freezing. Thus the canvases must be hung, and tied to a point some distance below the bottom of exterior columns. Salt-hay can also be placed around the column bottoms. In extremely cold weather the floor below the bottoms of the exterior columns in question is surrounded by canvas and a salamander or oil-burning space heater is placed on the floor at each. Follow carefully the usual methods for fire protection.

10. If the monolithic walls are carried up with the structure, the floor where the wall is being poured and the floor immediately below are both canvased in. Salamanders or heaters should be placed on both floors. Build heat holes through the wall being poured (about 10 x 10 in.) so that the heat can flow between the outside of the wall form and the canvas protection.

11. Keep a temperature record while the winter weather protection is in place, giving the following information:

Date, time, and specific place.
Temperature outside the building.
Temperature at bottom of exterior columns.
Temperature at bottom of floor slab forms.
Temperature under canvas covering slab.
Temperature of concrete at placement.

12. In extremely cold weather canvases should be placed over the top of a floor slab concrete pour. A framework to support the canvas is erected and tied to the column bond bars. If the columns were poured on a previous day, clamp 2 x 6 wood pieces to the column steel (if a steel building) or to the column bond bars (if a concrete building) before pouring fresh concrete. Then place 4 x 6 timbers from column to column after the concrete has been poured, on top of the 4 x 6 timbers. Lay 3 x 4s spanning from 4 x 6, or lay light wood skeleton panels, previously made up. This framework should be about 18 to 24 in. above the slab. Install heat holes in the floor forms and concrete, so that the heat below the slab flows into the area above the slab. The framework and canvas cannot be placed until the floor has been troweled, if it is a monolithic floor. Remove the canvas protection from the top of slab about 3 to 4 days after pouring.

13. The job superintendent should inspect the location of all salamanders, both coke- and oil-burning heaters, and the condition of the canvas before he leaves the job at night. If possible, he should visit the job once each night to assure himself that the watchmen are on the alert.

Figures 49–51 show some types of winter weather protection.

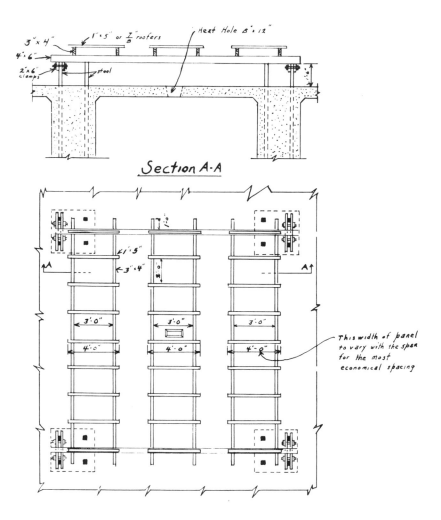

Fig. 49 Support for canvas covering.

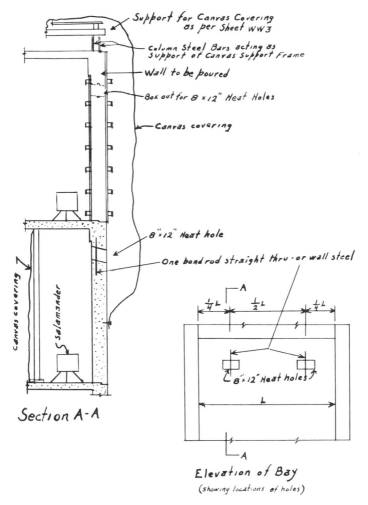

Fig. 50 Section and elevations showing protection of monolithic walls.

23. Radiant Heating Pipes in Floors

The layout of the pipes should be surveyed and recorded, particularly in the position of new door openings. Since the door bucks must be anchored to the floor, it is important that no radiant heat pipes pass under the door positions. If the anchors for the door bucks pierced the heat pipes, repairs would be very costly.

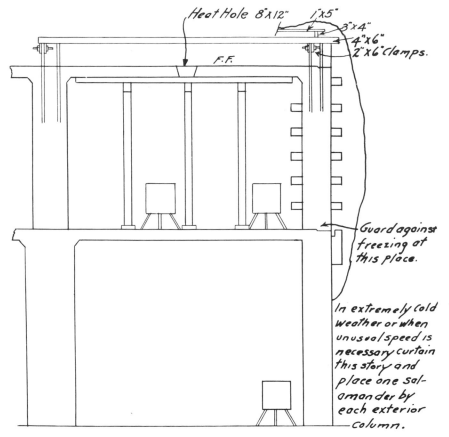

Fig. 51   Support for canvas covering at exterior columns.

After radiant heating pipes have been installed on the floor forms (and prior to placing the concrete) fill around and over these pipes.

Also before concreting around radiant heating pipes, the pipes must be tested under air or water pressure, to find out whether there are any leaks in the installation, or any defective pipes. It is very important that these tests be made, because it will prove very costly in terms of time and money to trace a leak after the concrete has set.

24.   Floor Hardeners (When Called for)

The use of a floor hardener is recommended to improve the durability of concrete floors and to make them dustproof. The floor hardener should have a low viscosity to ensure penetration of the material into the concrete surface. It should react chemically with the free lime and calcium carbonate in the Portland cement to form a hard, insoluble filler within the surface pores of the concrete. Floors should not have any plaster, paint, or other foreign substances on their surfaces when the hardener is applied.

Types of floor hardeners now on the market include the following:

1. *Zinc-Magnesium Fluosilicate.* This material seems to be the best floor hardener: 20% zinc salts and 80% magnesium salts are used in a solution of one pound of fluosilicates.
2. *A. C. Horns, Hornolith.*
3. *A. C. Horns, Hornstone.*
4. *L. Sonnenborn and Sons, Lapidolith.* This is a very good floor hardener.
5. *Sodium Silicates (water glass).* Water must be added before use, to ensure penetration of the concrete surface.
6. *Aluminum sulfate.* This material is not entirely satisfactory.
7. *Zinc Sulfate.* This material is not as efficient as other floor hardeners.

Checklist

1. Design mix.
2. Reinforcing details.
3. Form drawings, if required.
4. Material samples.
5. Elevations and layout.
6. Sleeves for trades.
7. Reinforcing placement.
8. Special attachments, inserts, and anchor bolts.
9. Form stability.
10. Location of expansion joints.
11. Weather (heat may be required).
12. Proper equipment for pour.
13. Notify inspection personnel

4

Masonry

1. Preparation

Preparation for the start of the masonry is much the same as for concrete; access is of prime importance. Daily delivery of masonry supplies necessitates easy access. Access to an area for storage, or to stack bricks that may come weeks before they may be needed. When a fixed hoist is used, a pad must be poured for the hoist tower and the necessary platforms built. All must be coordinated with the masonry contractor, foreman, or superintendent. In most cases the hoist is supplied by the masonry contractor and taken over by the general contractor when most of the masonry work is completed. On low buildings a rubber-tired lift may be used for servicing the brick layer.

It is important to see that the perimeter on the building is backfilled to just below the brick seat elevation.

Exterior scaffolding used depends on the type of building. Pipe or wood scaffold is used on bearing wall construction, hanging scaffold from multistorey concrete or steel framed building (Fig. 52).

Other trades are required to work along with the bricklayer as he proceeds to erect the exterior walls. It is important that these trades be properly coordinated, since dampproofing and spandrel flashing must be installed as the walls are erected (Figs. 53 and 54). Lintels must receive their final adjustment as the masonry proceeds upward (see Chapter 5). The line and grades must be established for the layout man to begin his important work of establishing coursing and building line limits.

To keep movement of material at a minimum, the plant for the masonry contractor should be located conveniently. The center of the exterior of the

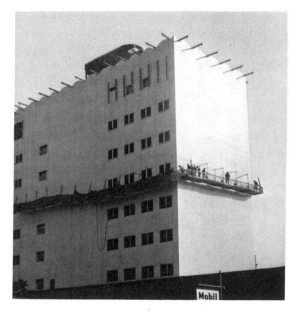

Fig. 52 Bricklayers washing down face brick from the scaffold used to erect the brick.

building is usually the location for the hoist. The hoisting tower, when used, is lined up with the windows, so that a minimum of patching is required when the hoist is removed (see Fig. 55 for loading of floors).

This, of course, is the ideal location, but some characteristic of the building might preempt this choice. It is important to check the drawings to see what type of construction may be involved at each landing. It may be fine for the mason to locate at this point, but having him there may be disadvantageous to the future progress of the job, since the hoist will remain until the building elevator is in use.

2. The Masonry Work

Once the mason begins, it is important to check to see that the brick ties, masonry, reinforcement, expansion joints, weep holes, and any special accessories called for by the drawings and specifications are not omitted.

Exterior masonry walls are usually of solid, cavity, or veneer construction. Cavity wall construction requires the closest attention. The cavity

Fig. 53 Bricklayer laying out wall on top of spandrel flashing over brick ledge.

must be kept free of mortar. A stick, called a snot stick, is placed in the cavity and pulled up as the wall is erected, removing the excess mortar dropped into the cavity. The stick is raised up and supported at each level of the wall ties (drip ties) that tie the outer layer of brick with the inside layer of block.

Some specifications require mortar to be tested for strength—since mortar is mixed on the job, it is important to take these tests regularly.

Masonry passing in front of concrete columns and spandrel beams is tied back to inserts cast into the concrete. The removable filler in the inserts should be removed before the mason reaches them, however. It is important not only that the dovetail anchor be installed in them but that the mortar also fill the slot.

Care must be taken to see that masonry openings (dimensions for windows, louvers, and door frames) not built into the wall are maintained. In some cases, templates are built to ensure the proper opening.

Built-in items in the masonry must be provided as needed. Delays are caused by the absence of door bucks, when these are needed by the mason, and installing the bucks at a later date is costly, as well.

Fig. 54 The bricklayer's layout man, marking courses on the column. Note spandrel flashing on the brick ledge. It continues around the corner and up the face of the column.

Fig. 55 Masonry stacked on the floors above as the bricklayer begins closing in the exterior of the building.

3. Coordination among Trades

The electrical and mechanical trades having items built into the masonry must be advised at all times of the mason's plan of work (see Chapters 15 and 16). The coordination of the trades is the prime function of the general contractor superintendent.

The masonry wall layout of interior partitions is a cooperative venture between the mason contractor and the carpenter setting the door bucks. (See Chapter 6 for the installation of the door bucks.) Once the bucks have been set and secured, the mason must take care not to move them. A check should be taken as the wall is erected for plumbness and racking of the bucks.

4. Cleanup

Cleanup is a major headache during the progress of the job. It is important that the mason's rubble be removed as soon as possible. The mason will scrape the floors and put the mortar and rubble in piles each day. If the rubble is not removed within a day or two, it will harden, requiring an electric hammer or sledge hammers to break up the piles. Job conditions dictate how the rubble is to be removed (Fig. 56).

When the exterior of the building is completed, the masonry is washed down. The specifications dictate the material that can be used. After the masonry has been cleaned and the scaffolds removed, it is important to clean around the perimeter and to bring the area to a finished grade or close to it (Fig. 52).

5. A Few Masonry Do's and Don't's

Masonry material stored on the job site should always be covered. The top of the masonry wall should be covered at the end of each day's work.

Masonry material should always be stored on platforms or skids so that the bricks, and so on, do not come in contact with the ground. Equipment must be washed down each day.

Fig. 56 Rubbish chute used to discharge the masonry rubbish into a truck or container. Note spandrel flashing along bottom face of parapet.

6. *Natural and Cast Stone*

Cast stone is usually reserved for sills, lintels, and coping. Natural stone, in addition to the uses above, is used as finished surfaces on the interior and exterior of the building.

There are many types of stone in each class—marble, granite, limestone, and sandstone. The architect, of course, specifies the type of stone.

7. *Erection of Stone Work*

Erection of the stone work is a trade by itself. The dowels, tie wire, and special ties, to secure the stone work to the backup material, usually are supplied by the general contractor and installed by the stone setter. In most cases nonferrous material is used; thus it is important to consult the specifications before ordering material.

Fig. 57 Stone setters preparing to put keystone in small window arch. On the right, a carpenter is starting to frame up structure, to support erection of large stone arch.

Limestone, when erected for exterior use, should be covered at the top every night because dampness getting behind the wall will cause discoloration of the stone. When erecting masonry backup for limestone, nonstaining mortar must be used.

Close attention to the specifications is important, for each stone has its own characteristics. Literature on the characteristics of each type of stone can be obtained from the association representing the stone involved. Figure 57 shows the erection of stone work.

Checklist

1. Material samples.
2. Mortar design mix.
3. Wall sample, if required.
4. Provide storage and work area.
5. Layout and coursing.
6. Built-In items.

7. Clearances.
8. Specified material installed.
9. Tieback to structure.
10. Expansion joints.
11. Plumbness.

5

Structural Steel and Miscellaneous Metal

"Structural steel and miscellaneous iron" covers a wide variety of items. The structural steel section of the specifications, of course, is limited to the major structural components of the building. Separate sections deal with steel decking and steel joists, but the Miscellaneous Iron section covers everything from cast iron frames for manholes to pipe supports for locker room benches. If an item does not appear on a drawing in the specifications, it is usually listed in this section, if metal is involved.

1. Structural Steel

Preparation for the erection of the structural steel framework begins with the checking of the anchor bolt locations and elevation at the column locations. The steel erector sends out his surveyor to check the existing field conditions before dispatching his erection crew. If the anchor bolts are too far off, they may have to be removed and expansion bolts substituted. Those that can be adjusted are moved and made ready for the erector before he arrives on the site. The distance from the bottom of the base plate to the concrete is indicated, to show how high the base plate must be shimmed. Once the columns have been set, framed, and plumb, the base plates are grouted in place. Sometimes a leveling plate is set and grouted in place before the erectors arrive on the site. Space must be made available for unloading and shaking out the steel as it arrives on the job site. If the building occupies the entire site, permits must be taken out to erect from the street.

Safety requirements involving the crews are carried out and enforced by the crews themselves. Protection of the public is left in the hands of the superintendent. Sidewalk bridges, rerouting of traffic, and other protection should be established and maintained during the erection of the steel. Once the steel frame has been erected and bolted, the only adjustments necessary are the setting of the lintels to line and, in cooperation with the masonry contractor, adjustment in elevation to accommodate the coursing. Figures 58–62 are typical scenes in the steel erection process.

2. Miscellaneous Metal

Many of the miscellaneous metal items are installed in cooperation with other trades. The main items that are included are as follows:

1. Stairs.
2. Railings, steel and aluminum.
3. Loose lintels.

Fig. 58 Pocket cut into the wall of an existing building, to receive new steel for an addition. Note large area to expedite the welding.

Fig. 59 Pockets cut into the side of an existing building, exposing the steel columns. The clip angles will be welded to the existing columns to receive the new beams. This cut was done before the steel erector came on the job with his crane and large crew to erect the structural steel.

Fig. 60 Bricklayers patching pockets when steel is in place.

Fig. 61 Erecting steel close into the building, bringing out the excavated material on the ramp used by the excavator.

4. Anchor bolts for all trades.
5. Cast iron covers for site work.
6. Frames and covers for pits.
7. Supports for air conditioning equipment.
8. Service walkways.
9. Supports for architectural trim.
10. Metal protection posts.

Stairs are installed as soon as possible. If the stairs are metal pan and the pans are not to be filled immediately, temporary wood tread should be installed.

It is important to have the loose lintels delivered to the job as soon as

Fig. 62   Erecting structural steel. Note access provided for trucks.

the mason starts work. They may be either cut to length or delivered long and cut on the job as required. Lintels that have some fabrication, such as bolted back to back, are delivered fabricated.

Many of the items above must be embedded in the concrete (sleeves for railings, anchor bolts, frames for pit covers, etc.). The items and shop drawings must be ready and available when needed. This requires the superintendent to be aware of what is needed. The subcontractor has a responsibility to see that these items are in place, but the superintendent must see at all times that they are available.

Proper installation of supports for air conditioning equipment depends on the information received from the HVAC contractor. This is usually expedited through the home office, but the superintendent should know the status of the shop drawings.

For all items supplied by the miscellaneous subcontractor, shop drawings will have been approved before fabrication. These usually show any field preparation required for the installation. The superintendent should be well aware of these requirements and should make sure that the trades involved have copies in the field. Too often the subcontractor's office has the information, but it is not given to the field. A check should also be made to see that the latest revisions of the drawings are in the field.

Checklist

1. Shop drawings.
2. Anchor bolt layout.
3. Coordination among trades.
4. Crane permits, if required.
5. Protection of public.
6. Access to site.
7. Plumbness of structure.
8. Adjustment for other trades.
9. Built-in items.
10. Painting requirements.

6

Carpentry and Millwork

The carpentry and millwork section of the specifications covers several phases during the construction of a building. The carpentry involved in the formwork for concrete is covered in Chapter 3.

1. Carpentry

The carpentry work includes the following areas:

1. Protection: barricades, temporary steps, and so on.
2. Wood blocking and grounds for other trades, such as for millwork, casework, roofing, and plaster work.
3. Installation of door bucks and hardware.
4. Framing for wood studding and wood structures (Fig. 63).

2. Millwork

Principal millwork items are as follows:

1. Wood windows and doors.
2. Wood counters.
3. Wood paneling.
4. Wood shelving.
5. Plastic laminated material.

Fig. 63 Carpenters raising a stud partition, fabricated on the floor, into its vertical position.

3. Lumber and Door Bucks

Lumber to be used depends on the specification. In fireproof buildings, fire-retardant lumber is used. Lumber embedded in masonry, concrete, and for roof blocking, wolminized treated lumber is generally used.

Because the setting of the door bucks is of major importance, methods commonly used for their installation are given below.

Door bucks are located in conjunction with the trades involved in the construction of the wall. In all types of wall, after the buck has been set in position and leveled by shims or adjustable clip angles, if necessary, the buck is secured to the floor. In masonry walls, after the buck has been set plumb, the head is secured to the ceiling or to the floor by temporary wood struts and blocking. It is secured to maintain plumbness in both directions. While the mason erects the wall, the temporary struts and blocking are removed by him after the wall has been built scaffold high and is stiff enough to hold the buck secure as masonry work on the wall around the buck is completed. The carpenter should make up several spreader sticks for the mason to set when he begins to block in the buck, to prevent bellying in of the buck jambs. When studded walls are erected, the bucks are set plumb and attached to the studding. The studding is doubled up at the head and jambs. The bucks described above are welded frames and must be erected with the wall. In some cases masonry openings are provided for bucks secured to the jamb of the openings. In such instances a subbuck may be secured to the masonry with anchor bolts, and the door buck screwed in place against the subbuck. Knockdown bucks are also used and can be installed in trimmed openings both in masonry and studded walls. Knockdown bucks, of course, have an obvious advantage.

Doors and hardware are usually installed after all the wet trades are complete. Wood doors should not be brought on the job until the building has dried out.

4.   Cutouts

With hollow metal, cutouts and holes for the locks and hinges (butts) are shop cut and shop drilled, and tapped for their screws. Screw holes for closures, kick plates, and panic bolts, and face plates for locks, are drilled and tapped in the field. Self-tapping screws can also be used, but drilling and tapping is preferred.

Wood doors that are shop cut for butts and locks can now be purchased. In most cases wood doors are prepared on the job, however. Special tools are available for routing out for butts, and so on.

5.   Framing

Framing for wood structures is a subject all its own. The lumber industry issues many pamphlets that can be consulted. The superintendent should be aware of the necessary metal fastenings and accessories involved in each particular structure. Laminated beam and girder construction has become an important new building technique with many new uses.

6.   Checking on Millwork

Millwork usually is delivered to the job in sections. Making a mistake of overcutting can be very costly, and the superintendent should be familiar with the shop drawings before assembly. The millwork shop drawing should also be available during the early stages of construction, to ensure that the proper clearances are left and embedded grounds are installed where called for. Field measurements are taken for some items of millwork before manufacture: field and job conditions determine whether field measurements are taken or clearance dimensions are held. Wherever possible, it is preferable to deliver fully assembled items to the job.

Checklist

1. Shop drawings.
2. Material samples and color samples.
3. Field measurements.
4. Material requirements.
5. Material delivery.
6. Coordination among trades.
7. Dampness conditions.
8. Proper storage of millwork.
9. Protection of installed items.

7

Roofing, Sheetmetal, Insulation, Sealants, Spandrel Flashing, Waterproofing, and Dampproofing

1. Roofing

Today there are many new types of roofing system, and the superintendent should familiarize himself with the system specified. Each system has its special preparation requirements, which must be met before the roofer begins. The roof surface should be thoroughly inspected for snots, projections, and smoothness, and necessary corrections should be made before the roofer comes on the job. The roof should be clean and dry before any roofing material is installed. I have found that a well-prepared surface is a cue to a leakproof roof.

2. Sheetmetal

Sheetmetal work associated with the roof takes many forms: through-wall flashing in conjunction with cap flashing, flashing under stone coping, pitch pockets, sleeves for pipe penetrations, gravel stops, flashing around roof drains, and counterflashing are some of the items included in this section of the specification for a typical roof. Metal flashing may also be used for spandrel. Flashing materials used are copper, stainless steel, aluminum, and lead-coated copper.

3. *Insulation and Sealants*

Requirements for the insulation for the roof as well as other uses throughout the building construction are contained in this section of the specifications. The roofer installs the roofing insulation.

Perimeter insulation is called for below grade on foundation walls and under slabs on grade. Usually if the concrete is poured against the insulation, the concrete contractor installs it. If placed against the concrete after the forms are stripped, an appropriate trade installs the insulation.

Insulation in cavity wall may be called for and must be installed, in cooperation with the masonry contractor.

Interior insulation in ceiling and walls is installed as detailed or as specified. The specifications should be carefully read, since the insulation may be called for in the specification only, and not shown on the drawings.

Sealants are installed throughout the job where expansion is expected to occur. A few of the major areas to be caulked are around exterior, windows, and door bucks, and sealing expansion joints in masonry and concrete. The type of sealant depends on the use and is spelled out in the specification. Caulking joints should be well cleaned and dry before sealing. Sealant should be installed in moderate temperatures for easiest application. See *Construct Sealants and Adhesives,* by John P. Cook (Wiley 1970).

4. *Waterproofing*

Waterproofing takes many forms, again depending on what is specified. The surfaces to be covered should be clean, smooth, and dry for all types of waterproofing except for cement waterproofing, such as Ionite. A damp and rough surface is required. The surface is usually bushhammered to achieve the roughness required.

5. *Dampproofing*

Dampproofing, usually applied to the inside face of the exterior walls or exterior face below grade, requires a minimum of preparation (Fig. 64).

Fig. 64   Dampproofing applied to the exterior wall to be backfilled. Areaway walls are not dampproofed.

It is applied by trowel or brush. The interior dampproofing is usually hidden by a finished wall. Masonry walls that have become porous, with dampness showing through on the inside wall, can be coated on the exterior with a clear dampproofing compound. Before this is done, cracks must be cleaned out and repaired, and loose mortar joints cut out and repointed. Some brick may have to be removed and replaced before the dampproofing material is applied.

Checklist

1. Shop drawings.
2. Material samples.
3. Material requirements.
4. Preparation for installation.
5. Coordination among trades.
6. Protection after installation.

8

Hollow Metal, Hardware, Windows, Aluminum and Stainless Steel Entrances, Curtain Walls, and Glass and Glazing

1. Hollow Metal and Hardware

Hollow metal (HM) and hardware are the first items ordered for the job. Unless the specifications call for standard manufactured bucks and off-the-shelf hardware, delivery time is lengthy. The doors and bucks cannot be fabricated until the hardware schedule, prepared by the hardware supplier, has been approved. The bucks are manufactured first and can be fabricated and delivered about 2 to 4 weeks after the hardware has been approved. The doors usually follow 10 weeks later. The expediting of the respective schedules is most important. Questions asked of the field by these contractors should be answered immediately.

When hardware is delivered to the job, it should be checked immediately, then stored in a safe place. Though the cost of replacing lost hardware is significant, the cost due to the delay in the reordering and delivery is also very high in terms of labor and may delay the completion of the job.

It is important to have the hardware supplier mark the packaged hardware by the item number and hardware sets for easy identification for installation. The door bucks and doors come to the job tagged for easy identification.

2. *Windows*

Windows can be delivered to the job glazed or unglazed depending on job conditions. The shop drawing shows the attachments necessary for installation. Where windows are installed in masonry openings, the clearances and blocking are shown in detail, and the superintendent must watch closely to be sure that there are no discrepancies in the dimensions of clearances left and windows supplied. Attachment of sills and trim are shown and must be coordinated with all trades involved.

3. *Aluminum and Stainless Steel Doors and Frames*

Aluminum and stainless steel doors and frames, commonly called "store fronts" by the trade, are installed in trimmed openings. In most cases the openings are field measured before fabrication. If recessed door closures are floor mounted, a recess in the floor is required for the hardware. The frame and doors should be protected after erection. Scratches on the metal are impossible to repair.

4. *Curtain Wall Construction*

Curtain wall construction has become a very important addition to building construction. Erection of the curtain wall requires many different types of fastening. Here again, cooperation among trades is important. Clip angles installed on the structural steel and inserts in concrete must be installed from the shop drawing layout supplied by the curtain wall contractor and incorporated on the shop drawings of the subcontractor affected. The coordination of the drawings is followed through the home office, but the field coordination falls into the hands of the superintendent. Before the curtain wall contractor arrives on the job, a check should be made with his engineering personnel for any interferences. Any required changes must be made before the erectors arrive on the job.

5.   Glass and Glazing

The glazing of exterior windows should follow closely the completed exterior wall. Glazing of interior borrowed lights, door lights, and glass partitions should be installed after the wall finishes have been completed and before painting. In all instances the frames must be cleaned and the removable stops made available to the glazer, if these are delivered separately.

After glazing, doors and partitions should be marked by tape or material that will not damage the glass. This is a safety requirement to prevent the workers from walking into the glass.

Checklist

1. Shop drawings.
2. Hardware schedule.
3. Material samples.
4. Material requirements.
5. Material delivery.
6. Secured storage for hardware.
7. Location and plumbness of door frames.
8. Preparation for special doors.
9. Preparation for window erection.
10. Mark glass doors and glass partitions for view.
11. Protection after erection.

9

*Finishing Trades**

1. *Lathing for Plaster Walls*

There are two basic materials for lathing: rock lath (perforated sheet rock) and steel lath, of which there are many types. Both are installed over wood or steel furring or studding; the type of material required is given in the specification. The manufacturers of these products publish very good product manuals complete with details of their products and installation procedures. This literature should be obtained for reference. Corner beads, stop beads, and expansion beads are installed with the lath. It is important that care be taken in their installation. A good plaster job depends to a large extent on properly installed beads, and no compromises should be made during this installation. A check should be made to be sure that all conduits, pipes, attachments for equipment are installed correctly before the installation of the final layer of lathing.

2. *Plaster*

Before starting any plaster work, check the beads. Correct any bead that is not set right and replace any damaged beads.

There are three types of plaster commonly used: gypsum, Portland cement, and vermiculite plaster. Plaster is applied on metal lath in three coats: the scratch coat, the brown coat, and the finish coat. On masonry,

---

* Interior partitions other than masonry are specified under this section; wood studding and furring is under carpentry.

the scratch coat may be eliminated and with Portland cement and vermiculite plaster; the brown coat may also be the finish coat. On small jobs the plaster is mixed on the floor near the work area. On large jobs a mixing area is centrally located, and the material transported vertically by a special hoist. Today most plaster is pumped, and the scratch and brown coats are sprayed on and leveled by troweling. The white finish coat for gypsum plaster is applied by trowel. No matter which system is used, plaster is a messy job. It is important that each day's work be followed up by cleanup and removal.

Grounds are installed in the plaster wall for attaching equipment and near the base of the wall, when called for, to provide a straight wall for rubber, tile, or terrazzo bases. Care must be exercised to line up the grounds with the beads. As stated before, a good plaster job depends on proper preparation.

3. Spray Fireproofing

Most modern buildings call for fireproofing of the structural steel by spray fireproofing. This is usually performed by the plastering contractor. Most specifications state the hour rating required. There are several spray fireproofing products on the market, each having different thickness requirements. Metal decks may require fireproofing spray if the concrete thickness is not adequate. It is important that the superintendent check with his subcontractor regarding the material to be used, the required thickness, and similar matters. He must find out from the local building department whether the product is approved, and the department's requirements. The engineer should also be consulted.

Installation of the spray fireproofing should be carried out before ducts and pipes are hung from the arch. Before the ceilings are installed, the fireproofing should be checked and patched wherever it has been damaged.

4. Drywall Partitions

Drywall is being used more and more to replace plaster. The sheet rock is applied to either wood or steel studding or furring. After the sheet rock has been secured, the joints are taped. Taping compounds come premixed, but they can be mixed on the job, as well. The compound is spread over the joint area; then the perforated tape is applied and additional passes of the compound are spread over the tape and smoothed over to create a jointless wall. The exposed tops of the fastening are also covered. A new method, the Imperial Plaster System, is basically a drywall system covered with a thin coat of plaster (see U.S. Gypsum, *Products and System Book*).

5.   *Movable Partitions*

Generally in office buildings some partitions in a large office room are movable metal partitions about 8 ft high, with a few posts secured to the ceiling for stability. The partitions should be installed as soon as the finish flooring material is laid. Partitions are not made stationary so that they can be repositioned to accommodate changes in the office layout pattern after construction is completed.

6.   *Hung Plaster Ceilings*

Plaster celings require lathing. A grid system of main runner carrying channels is suspended from the arch, and cross-furring channels are tied perpendicular to them to the main channels. The lath is then wire tied to the furring channels. The most important operation to check is the installation of the supporting channels: they must be level at the required elevation. Then the balance of the grid falls in place. If stop beads are called for along the perimeter of the walls, they should be set true and level. The superintendent should ensure the availability, when needed, of the plaster rings to be installed by the lathers for lighting fixtures and defusers; these rings are supplied by the respective trades. The plaster is applied in the same manner as on the walls.

7.   *Hung Acoustical Ceilings*

The two main types of hung acoustical ceiling are exposed "T" and concealed spline. There are two types of suspension: direct-hung, and one using carrier channels, supported directly from the arch and leveled as described for plaster hung ceilings. The acoustical ceiling is then hung from the carrier channels. The direct-hung ceiling is suspended directly from the arch by wire tied to the suspension system of the ceiling system used. The superintendent should obtain the manufacturer's literature of the ceiling system and familiarize himself with the method of installation.

It is important to have the literature sent to the electrical contractor, for each type of ceiling requires the electrical fixtures to be supplied with different types of attachment and trim. Most acoustical ceilings are affected by dampness, and this property should be checked with the ceiling manufacturer. If the ceiling is susceptible to dampness, the material should not be brought on the job while the wet trades are working or before the building has dried out.

8.   *Flooring*

Each of the many types of floor finish has its particular use. A few of the most common are discussed.

Resilient Floor

Vinyl asbestos tile (VAT) is the resilient flooring most commonly used today. It is most important that the surface that is to be installed over be completely dry, smooth, and level. In some cases the surface has to be corrected for proper installation; the following methods are the most widely used.

1.   *For Concrete.*   A latex base material is troweled over the repairable surface to a smooth and level finish. It is fast drying, and the flooring can be laid over within an hour. The process is known as flash patching.
2.   *For Wood Floors.*   Where the floor is very bad and cannot be repaired with only minimum replacement of the existing floor, the floor is covered with an underlayment material such as plywood or hardboard. The VAT is then installed on the underlayment.

Carpeting

The preparation for carpeting is the same as for resilient floor.

Terrazzo Floors: Floating, Bonded, and Epoxy Types

Another type of floor is terrazzo. For the floating-type terrazzo the installation, the structural slab should be kept down to about 4 in. A 2½ in. bed of sand and cement is then spread over the rough slab, followed by the terrazzo floor, about 1½ in. thick. Metal dividing strips are set before the terrazzo is poured, in a pattern specified by the architect. Each dividing strip must run from wall to wall, since these strips are installed in the location where the terrazzo is likely to crack.

Terrazzo floors should be placed by a reputable terrazzo contractor who has had years of experience with terrazzo floors. These floors cannot be installed by inexperienced men.

In a bonded terrazzo floor the structural slab should be washed down with water under pressure, remove the foreign particles that are on the slab. About 1¼ in. of terrazzo is then poured on top of the structural slab, after the dividing strips have been installed.

In both bonded and floating terrazzo floors the terrazzo is roped off and cured for 7 years. The floor should be washed before it is used.

Epoxy terrazzo is generally used to cover an existing concrete floor. This is a very practical flooring for existing buildings where there is little room between the bottom of the doors and the floor. Some firms specialize in epoxy floors. The epoxy mix is made up by a chemical company and mixed in a small mixer. First the existing floor is scrubbed clean; then dividing strips are installed. This type of terrazzo is placed, then ground, in the same manner in which the other terrazzo floors are placed. Epoxy terrazzo is about ¼ to ⅜ in. thick.

Wood Floors

There are two methods of laying wood floors. In one method metal wire anchors, used to secure the 2 x 4 beveled wood sleepers, are poured in the top of the structural concrete slab. The 2 x 4 wood sleepers are sometimes painted, dipped, or sprayed with creosote, which acts as a preservative. The sleepers are then installed. A long straightedge is used to make sure they are level, and the wood flooring is tocnailed into the sleepers. The wood floor is then scraped, sanded, treated, and covered with heavy paper until used.

The other type of wood floor is glued to the concrete slab, which must be very smooth or else the flooring will not lie level. This type of floor, called a parquet floor, consists of square wooden blocks made out of short pieces of wood flooring, about 6 to 8 in. long. The boards are glued and wired together so that they can never separate. The blocks are laid in an adhesive material spread on the floor. After the floor has been set up, it is scraped, sanded, and treated, the same as the other type of wood floor.

Quarry Tile Floors

Quarry tile floors are used in kitchens, dining rooms, terraces, and other locations where a hard floor that can be cleaned easily is required. A bed of sand and cement is placed over the rough structural floor. Then the back of the tile is coated with a mixture of water and cement, and the quarry tile is laid over the bed of sand and cement. Quarry tile is laid to a straight edge, with cement joints about ⅝ in. thick on all four sides of each quarry tile. The tile is pounded in place, and a straightedge is used to make sure that the floor is level. This floor is easy to clean, and quarry tile can be made acid resistant.

Ceramic Tile Floors and Walls

Ceramic finishes are used in bathrooms, kitchens, dining rooms, and so on. This tile is mounted on paper-backed sheets and is laid on a bed composed of sand and cement. The ceramic tile is laid down on top of this bed with the paper backing on top. After the tile has set, the paper backing is removed by washing it off the tile with water. The tile joints are then filled with a cement grout. Another method of installing the tile is called *thin-set*. An adhesive is used instead of the sand and cement bed.

Miscellaneous Flooring Systems

There are many types of floor finishes, as well as patented systems for industrial floors, gymnasiums, and hospitals. The superintendent should read the literature of the manufacturer of the flooring used, to be able to prepare the subfloor properly.

Where static electricity is a problem, conductive floors are called for. These floors have to be grounded, and coordination with the electrical contractor must be arranged.

9. *Painting*

No other trade receives more attention from the architect than painting. Paint colors are selected by the architect, and of course this must be done before the painter begins work. A check with the home office should be made early to ensure that the color selection is complete or is being expedited.

On the job, the superintendent should see that the walls present proper working conditions for the painter. Masonry walls should be free of snots and rough-tooled joints. Door bucks should be free of mortar, so that the painter only has to sand down the buck lightly. A moisture meter should be used to check masonry and plaster walls for dampness. The specifications on the paint manufacturer's literature will indicate the required readings.

Before he starts painting, the painter will fill cracks and do minor joint patching and sanding on sheet rock. After the prime coat has been applied some defects that were not corrected before starting show up through the prime coat and must be corrected before application of the second coat.

Be sure to verify that all coats specified are applied. It is important to see that the painter protects all unpainted surfaces, such as hardware and aluminum frames. Removing paint from these areas can be costly.

Holidays (areas not completely covered by the paint) and drips are eyesores to the architects. They should be watched for and corrected before the paint dries.

It is important to provide the painter with good lighting. Close control while the painter is working will pay off with a minimum of punch list items.

10. *Vinyl Wall Covering and Wallpaper*

Vinyl wall covering and wallpaper are becoming increasingly popular in commercial buildings and offices. Wall preparation is important, since any imperfections are exaggerated by the covering.

The wall coverings are usually installed by experienced workers in the trade. Some vinyl coverings are very expensive, and their replacements very costly. The paperhangers should have a clean, well-lighted area for their work.

11.   Temporary Heat

None of the finishing trades above can be installed in temperatures below freezing. Some require more heat than others. Temporary heat supplied by gas-fired salamanders, or space heaters will be sufficient for most of the wet trades. It is recommended that acoustical ceilings, resilient flooring, and painting not be installed until the permanent heating system of the building can be used. A malfunction of salamanders or space heaters may cause discoloration of the finished surfaces. If necessary, temporary electric heat may be used.

Checklist

1. Shop drawings, where required.
2. Material samples.
3. Paint schedule.
4. Coordination among trades.
5. Finish schedule posted in each room if a wide variety of finishes are specified.
7. Proper cleanup in work areas.
8. Proper scheduling among trades.
9. Protection of finishes.

10

Miscellaneous Specialties

A few of the common items specified under the "miscellaneous" section are as follows:

1. Folding, coiling, and sliding partitions.
2. Toilet partitions.
3. Toilet accessories.
4. Chalk boards and bulletin boards.
5. Signs and directories.
6. Telephone enclosures.
7. Lockers.
8. Access floors (computer floors).
9. Wardrobes.
10. Flagpoles.
11. Louvers.

The specifications require shop drawings or catalog cuts for each specialty item. It again becomes the responsibility of the superintendent to check supports called for in the shop drawings of items to be built into the walls and ceilings. Folding and sliding partitions, for example, may require steel supports, and these drawings should be coordinated with the miscellaneous steel contractor. Ceiling-hung toilet partitions may require additional ceiling supports. Flagpoles, depending on how they are supported, may require steel framing for their attachment, or concrete foundation.

Lockers may require concrete bases and/or wood blocking built into the walls, and bases for attachments. Louvers may require field measurements or the masonry openings held to a given size. Access floors are usually grounded and require coordination between the floor contractor and the electrical contractor.

All specialties have individual requirements and should be coordinated with the trade that is affected.

Checklist

1. Shop drawings.
2. Material samples.
3. Manufacturers' literature.
4. Coordination among trades.
5. Built-in items for installation.
6. Protective storage.
7. Protection after erection.

11

Equipment

The most important items under this the equipment section, and the ones the superintendent must closely coordinate, are as follows:

1. Casework—hospital and laboratory.
2. Food service equipment.
3. Detention equipment.
4. Loading dock equipment.
5. Library equipment.

1. Casework

"Casework," the term used for hospital and laboratory equipment, requires close coordination between the mechanical trades and the casework contractor. A penetration drawing supplied by the casework contractor shows the location of all service connections to his equipment, and the mechanical and electrical contractors must supply the necessary sleeves or holes in floors and service to meet the equipment service requirements. Since some penetration drawings locate the floor penetrations and others locate connections, close coordination is required in case allowances must be made for offsets.

The casework contractor may neglect to take into account structural conditions that may necessitate rerouting of piping. A close check of the equipment details should show the mechanical contractor how to offset his piping. If there is no solution, however, the equipment may have to be rearranged or altered. Close coordination among the trades is a must. When the equipment arrives on the job, it is too late to begin checking.

Special plumbing fixtures supplied by the casework contractor and installed by the plumbing contractor should be turned over to the plumbing contractor as soon as received. In most cases, all contractors install the service and equipment together or closely follow up the casework contractor.

2. Food Service Equipment

Food service equipment has special requirements. Pads have to be built, and close tolerance of walls has to be maintained or field measurements taken. The food service contractor supplies the drawings for his pad requirements and mechanical service requirements. Pad dimensions are finished dimensions. If a terrazzo base or quarry tile base is required, allowance should be made for its installation.

Cutouts are usually supplied in the counters for electrical service. It is important that these dimensions be held and that electrical receptacles shown diagrammatically on the electrical contractor's engineer's drawings be located from the food service equipment drawings, rather than being scaled off.

Fixtures supplied by the food service contractor and installed by the mechanical trades should be coordinated so that all is ready at the proper time.

3. Detention, Loading Dock, And Library Equipment

Detention, loading dock, and library equipment all require that special attachments be built into the previously built construction. Grounds, embedded steel angles, special plates, and inserts for erection are some of the minimal requirements. The shop drawing, again, must be consulted to coordinate with the necessary trades to properly prepare for the erection.

Delivery of all the equipment above requires special attention. All are finished products and should be protected against damage during delivery and after erection. Proper and safe storage space should be provided before erection. Items made of wood *should not be stored in damp areas*. After erection, rooms housing the equipment should be locked to keep out all unauthorized persons.

Checklist

1. Shop drawings.
2. Penetration drawings.
3. Manufacturers' literature.
4. Material samples.
5. Coordination among trades.
6. Built-in items for installation.
7. Protective storage before installation.
8. Protection after installation.

12

Furnishings

A few items that concern the superintendent in the furnishings section are listed below:

1. Venetian blinds.
2. Shades.
3. Draperies.
4. Public seating.
5. Mats.

These items sometimes require special built-in support. For Venetian blinds, shades, and draperies blocking may have to be attached to the ceiling or structural supports. The furnishings are then attached to the blockings. Public seating may call for the installations of special brackets or anchor bolts in the concrete when poured. Mats often require recesses and accompanying embedded frames.

All furnishing received on the job should be provided with proper and clean storage space. Rooms should be locked after installation, since this is usually the final finishing touch. Again, no wood furnishing should be brought into a damp building.

Checklist

1. Shop drawings.
2. Material samples.
3. Manufacturers' literature.

4. Coordination among trades.
5. Built-in items for installation.
6. Protective storage.
7. Protection after erection.

13

Special Construction

The section covering special construction contains a wide variety of special equipment provided in special types of buildings. A few of the items are listed below:

1. Radiation protection.
2. Insulated cold rooms.
3. Saunas.
4. Swimming pools.
5. Steam bath equipment.
6. Solar energy systems.

1. Special Considerations

All the special equipment construction involves the preparation of shop drawings, and all items must receive approval from the architect or engineer before any equipment arrives on the job. All work is done by specialists in the field. Again, the superintendent must follow through to ensure the necessary coordination among other trades on the job. Radiation protection requires special attention.

2. Radiation Protection

Material for radiation protection comes in several forms; all, of course, involve lead. The materials are as follows:

1. Lead sheets.
2. Lead-faced block.
3. Lead-coated sheet rock.

Lead sheets are attached to wood studding using lead nails. The sheets come prepared for overlapping to prevent radiation leakage and are installed by the carpenter.

Lead-faced block is installed by the mason. The block joints are made to overlap. Lead-coated sheet rock is installed by the carpenter with lead attachment and overlapping joints.

Doors and bucks intended for installation in the wall are lead lined also, and are purchased in this condition.

Checklist

1. Shop drawings.
2. Material samples.
3. Manufacturers' literature.
4. Coordination among trades.
5. Built-in items for installation.
6. Protective storage.
7. Protection after erection.

14

Conveying Equipment

The conveying equipment section includes the following items:

1. Elevators.
2. Moving stairs.
3. Moving walks.
4. Dumbwaiters.
5. Material lifts.
6. Material conveyors.

All the equipment above requires special attachment to the structures and service from other trades. The superintendent again is responsible for proper coordination.

The elevator contractor supplies special inserts to be installed in the concrete for his rail supports. Shop drawings from the equipment contractors show locations of anchor bolts and special steel supports, as well as electrical service and clearance requirements. It is important to consult the trades involved to ensure that they will meet these conditions.

The superintendent should bear in mind the size of the equipment, since proper access must be provided. It may be necessary to leave down walls and build them after the equipment is in place. Elevator hoisting equipment supports are built into the surrounding slab and the slab is poured after the equipment has been put in place.

When a hydraulic elevator is called for, the shaft for the piston is drilled and installed during the construction of the foundation, when access is easy for the drilling equipment. In alteration projects, special equipment is used to get into the tight spots.

Figure 65 illustrates the installation of conveying equipment in a factory.

Fig. 65   Conveying equipment installed in a factory.

Checklist

1. Shop drawings.
2. Material samples.
3. Manufacturers' literature.
4. Coordination among trades.
5. Built-in items for installation.
6. Protective storage.
7. Protection after erection.

15

Plumbing, Heating, Ventilation, and Air Conditioning

All mechanical trades are involved in a construction project from the first shovel in the ground to completion. Cooperation of these trades among themselves and all contractors on the job is essential. One of the most important job of the general contracting superintendent is to see that harmony exists among trades. This is no easy task, but once it has been achieved, the superintendent is assured of a good job.

1. Plumbing

Water on a job site is one of the first services to be brought in. All efforts must be made to provide this service as soon as possible. Until water is piped in, hydrants in the street are used, if available.

The plumber supplies drawings for the location of sleeves set in the concrete. He supplies the sleeves to the concrete contractor to set, or he may set them himself. The superintendent should check very closely to see that the sleeves are installed.

As outlined in Chapter 1, integrated drawings indicate the location of the plumbing lines in conjunction with the other trades. These drawings should be checked against the locations of lines as the installation proceeds. The plumbing contractor usually installs his piping before ducts are installed. Elevation becomes as important as location.

Most pipes in multistory buildings are located in pipe chases and branch off at each floor to the fixtures. The pipe installation should be closely monitored to see that the concealed pipes are within the wall lines. It sometimes becomes necessary to increase the thickness or location of the wall to accommodate the piping. The architect must be informed of any changes required and his approval requested.

After submission and approval of equipment and material to be incorporated, the superintendent should keep a constant vigil to see that these requirements are met. If a change is made, for reasons of delivery or job conditions, the architect should be advised and approval of the new schedule received before work is begun.

Plumbing drawings are schematic, and the location of equipment, cleanouts, access panels, and so on, should be closely attended to for problems of interference and accessibility.

The plumber should be kept well aware of all planned scheduling so that his presence will not delay any slab pours, or closing in of wall or ceilings. Where tests are required, they must be completed before the piping is enclosed.

2. Heating, Ventilation, and Air Conditioning (HVAC)

Usually one subcontractor is responsible for the HVAC trades.

When air conditioning is involved, the first major task of the contractor is to prepare drawings of his duct work, based on field measurements taken by a field sketcher. If the specifications call for integrated drawings, arrangements must be made to meet with the mechanical and electrical contractor to prepare them (see Chapter 1). Once the integrated drawings have been approved, all the contractors can proceed with their insert and sleeve location drawings, if required.

If the equipment ordered for air conditioning and heating is not standard, delivery dates must be monitored carefully. The equipment drawings should be checked for size against access into the building and equipment rooms. Boilers may have to be rigged into the boiler room before the first floor slab is poured. Walls may have to be left down for large delivery items.

Most equipment on the roof is supported on special pre-fabricated curbs. It is important to see that they are delivered in time for the roofing contractor when installing the roofing.

The requirements for the support of the fans and air conditioning equipment on the roof should be coordinated with the steel contractor. This is done usually by the office personnel, but the superintendent should be aware of the progress as it affects the progress of the job.

All the do's and don't's for plumbing hold true for the heating piping.

Duct installation should follow the approved shop drawings. Any field changes can radically affect the other trades.

There are many systems of air conditioning and controls. The superintendent should familiarize himself with the system used.

When a pneumatic control system is used, the system is kept under pressure and closely watched while the finishing trades are at work, since the tubing used is easily penetrated. If a drop in pressure is observed, a leak can easily be traced by a supervisor who knows where the men are working. This method is also used when a plumber has installed oxygen lines in hospital construction.

Before the air conditioning system is accepted by the engineer, several tests on equipment and operation must be performed; the last of these is the balancing of the system. If called for, this is usually performed by a certified balancing contractor, who adjusts and certifies the system.

Every effort should be made to complete the heating system as soon as possible, to permit use of the building facilities for temporary heat for the finishing trades (see Chapter 9).

3. Sprinklers

Sprinkler systems are installed in many buildings depending on the section of the country, they may be installed by plumbers or steamfitters or by both, the plumber bringing in the water service and the steamfitters installing the system after the meter. Two systems are used: a dry system, which must be used in unheated buildings, and a wet system. The sprinkler systems are generally laid out by the sprinkler contractor, and once the drawings have been approved, a minimum of change should be allowed unless engineering approval is obtained. The electrical contractor becomes involved with the sprinkler systems alarm controls. When the system is installed above a ceiling, drops are provided that extend below the ceiling construction. These are cut to size when the ceilings are finished, and the heads are installed with the necessary trim.

It should be noted that the different functions of the mechanical sections are covered by separate trade unions. The principal trades are plumbers, steamfitters, sheetmetal workers, insulators, wainwrights, and riggers.

Checklist

 1. Permits.
 2. Temporary water.
 3. Sleeve and insert location drawings.
 4. Coordination drawings, when required.
 5. Sheetmetal drawings.
 6. Shop drawings (equipment).
 7. Manufacturers' literature.
 8. Material samples.
 9. Material requirements.
10. Coordination among trades.
11. Check of sleeve locations before concrete is poured.
12. Check for omissions before walls close in pipes.
13. Test piping before walls close in pipes.
14. Check access door requirements.
15. Check out equipment.
16. Check out controls.
17. Balance out systems.
18. Complete instruction manuals.
19. Instruct owner on use of systems.
20. Clean equipment.

16

Electrical

Like the mechanical contractors, the electrical contractor is on the job from start to finish. Power must be brought on the site as soon as possible, and every effort must be made to hold the electrical contractor to his obligation to furnish this service. In most cases in new construction, the concrete contractor starts work with his own portable generator before the power is brought in.

The electrical contractor is responsible for all temporary lighting and power during the job. On multistory buildings, he must maintain, lighting on stairs and sidewalk bridges, with 24-hour service. He must provide and maintain the temporary and permanent power throughout the job.

The electrical contractor is involved in every phase of the work. Conduits are buried in concrete, encased in masonry supported by structural steel, hidden behind stud walls, and supported on ceiling channels. Electrical service supplied to the mechanical equipment controls wiring for HVAC systems and lighting installed from or recessed in ceilings.

Close cooperation among trades is most important. The superintendent should try hard to solve any conflicts immediately, to everyone's satisfaction.

Switch gear, motor control panels, lighting fixtures, and emergency generators are long lead time items. It is important that they be submitted for approval as soon as possible. This again is the home office's responsibility, but the superintendent should be aware of their progress and should know the scheduled delivery dates.

For equipment with electrical motors, supplied by other contractors, the motor starters and any other controls required must be turned over to the electrical contractor for installation. Sometimes in the case of a combination starter/disconnect switch, the electrical contractor may be required to supply the controls. The specifications should be checked for the appropriate supplier, so that the job is not delayed when the controls are supposed to be installed.

It is important to see that the electrical contractor has all the latest wiring diagrams for equipment supplied by other contractors and wired by the electrical contractor. If necessary, the superintendent should arrange meetings between the electrical contractor's foreman and the foreman or engineer associated with the equipment to be wired.

Checklist

1. Temporary power and light.
2. Sleeve and insert drawings.
3. Shop drawings.
4. Material samples.
5. Manufacturers' literature.
6. Coordination among trades.
7. Check location of conduits, sleeves, and stud up before slabs are poured.
8. Check walls being built to ensure that outlets and switches are in place.
9. Access door requirements.
10. Do not pull wires through conduit until roof is tight.
11. Protection from live wires.
12. Check control working.
13. Check equipment.
14. Mark all directories in panel boxes.
15. Instruct owner in use of special equipment.
16. Clean equipment.

17

Epilogue

As pointed out in the preface, the superintendent owes allegiance to his employer, the architect, the engineer, and the owner, and to his subcontractors. As his involvement grows in the everyday running of his job, he may find his task most difficult. The prime concern of his employer and subcontractors is to get the job done as economically as possible. The architect, engineer and owner want the best job obtainable for the money budgeted.

The preceding pages have said little about cost, but in every decision cost is a major concern. A job on schedule or ahead of schedule is always a cost saver. It is important that the superintendent keep a close rein on his men. Work assignments must be made with a minimum of lost time. Materials necessary for performance of the job must be available when and where needed, and in sufficient quantity. The subcontractors' work force must be encouraged to do their contractual share of the work efficiently, and their responsibilities in cleanup must be diligently pursued. Answers to questions on interpretation of the drawings and specifications must be answered expeditiously. Delay is costly.

It is impossible to determine the cost results of some decisions. Sometimes it is necessary to spend money to push the job by providing more service than would normally be given. If such an expenditure helps to bring the job in on time, or ahead of schedule, or to close in a building and get the roof completed before the winter weather sets in, it is money well spent.

Winter heat on a job is one factor that no one can figure correctly in advance. The superintendent should keep close watch to see that the money is spent wisely. Heating should be restricted to the areas being worked on, or where it is necessary to prevent the cold from damaging completed work.

Cleanup is another costly item that must be closely monitored. Dumping charges are costly, and trucks and containers must be utilized to their full capacity. Boxes and cartons should be broken down, and cans being thrown away should be filled with rubbish, if possible. Moving the rubbish to the discharge point should be efficiently handled. Chutes should be centrally located, and containers on wheels should be spotted in areas of work to cut down excess movement of rubbish. Each job is different, and the superintendent should make a point of knowing what is going on with his cleanup crews. Though this area may seem insignificant, neglect may be costly. Coordination of the removal of loaded containers and supply of empty containers must be closely watched. Having a good foreman or laborer in this area is most important.

Redoing work poorly or improperly installed is one of the prime causes of cost overruns. Though the subcontractor may bear the burden of the cost of the corrective work, time is lost and time is money.

Following closely the work in progress, and checking to see that all requirements are met as the job progresses, will cut the cost of the most expensive of nonproductive work, the "punch list" at the end of the job.

As repeated throughout the book, coordination is important. The superintendent must do everything in his power to meet the needs of all concerned. This is a monumental task. If all trades are cooperative, the superintendent's work is half done.

The superintendent must not act for the benefit of his employer only. Although his decisions must protect his employer's interest, they must be fair, there must be give and take on all sides. "Taking" only will cause dissension among the subcontractors on the job and will hurt the job in the long run.

The owner's representatives must be treated with respect, and discrepancies of opinions must be resolved in a businesslike manner. Firmness on the part of the superintendent when he is right will be respected by the owner's representative. It is important to maintain good relations with the owner's representative. He should be kept aware of all that is going on. This may be a nuisance sometimes, but it does pay off.

It is important that good records, readily available, be kept in the job office. The job staff should be advised of all changes, and they in turn should keep the superintendent up to date, each day, in their respective areas of responsibility. Communication is a very important factor in a well-run job.

The job meetings should be very informative. All areas of conflict should be discussed and solutions agreed on. Loose ends come back to haunt one.

Each superintendent will find his own way of running a job, but it is the end result that is important. Satisfying everyone on a job is almost impossible, but it is a goal to be reached.

Appendix

Industry Standards

Listed below are standards referred to in most specifications, along with the abbreviations commonly used for those references.

AA	Aluminum Association 750 Third Avenue; New York, NY 10017; 212/972-1800
AAMA	Architectural Aluminum Manufacturers Association 35 East Wacker Drive; Chicago, IL 60601; 312/782-8256
AASHTO	American Association of State Highway & Transportation Officials 341 National Press Building; Washington, DC 20004; 202/628-2438
ABPA	Acoustical and Board Products Association (Successor to AMA, IBI, and AIMA) 205 West Touhy Avenue; Park Ridge, IL 60068; 312/692-5178
ACEC	American Consulting Engineers Council 1155 15th Street, NW; Washington, DC 20005; 202/296-1780
ACI	American Concrete Institute P.O. Box 19150 Redford Station; Detroit, MI 48219; 313/532-2600
AGA	American Gas Association 1515 Wilson Boulevard; Arlington, VA 22209; 703/524-2000
AGC	The Associated General Contractors of America 1957 E Street, NW; Washington, DC 20006; 202/393-2040
AI	The Asphalt Institute Asphalt Institute Building; College Park, MD 20740; 301/927-0422
AIA	The American Institute of Architects 1735 New York Avenue; Washington, DC 20006; 202/785-7300
A.I.A.	American Insurance Association (Successor to NBFU) 85 John Street; New York, NY 10038; 212/433-4400
AISC	American Institute of Steel Construction, Inc. 1221 Avenue of the Americas; New York, NY 10020; 212/764-0440
AISI	American Iron and Steel Institute 1000 16th Street, NW; Washington, DC 20036; 202/223-9040

AITC   American Institute of Timber Construction
            333 West Hampden Avenue; Englewood, CO 80110; 303/761-3212

ANSI   American National Standards Institute
            (Successor to USASI and ASA)
            1430 Broadway; New York, NY 10018; 212/868-1220

APA   American Plywood Association
            119 A Street; Tacoma, WA 98401; 206/272-2283

ASAHC   American Society of Architectural Hardware Consultants
            See Door and Hardware Institute—DHI

ASC   Adhesive and Sealant Council
            2350 East Devon Avenue; Des Plaines, IL 60018; 312/296-1166

ASHRAE   American Society of Heating, Refrigerating & Air-Conditioning
              Engineers, Inc.
            345 East 47th Street; New York, NY 10017; 212/644-7953

ASME   American Society of Mechanical Engineers
            345 East 47th Street; New York, NY 10017; 212/6800

ASTM   American Society for Testing and Materials
            1916 Race Street; Philadelphia, PA 19103; 215/299-5400

AWI   Architectural Woodwork Institute
            5055 South Chesterfield Road; Arlington, VA 22206; 703/671-9100

AWPA   American Wood-Preservers' Association
            1625 Eye Street, NW; Washington, DC 20006; 202/331-1382

AWPB   American Wood Preservers Bureau
            2772 South Randolph Street; Arlington, VA 22206; 703/931-6377

AWPI   American Wood Preservers Institute
            1651 Old Meadow Road; McLean, VA 22090; 703/893-4005

AWS   American Welding Society, Inc.
            2501 NW 7th Street; Miami, FL 33125; 305/642-7090

BHMA   Builders Hardware Manufacturers Association
            60 East 42nd Street; New York, NY 10017; 212/682-8142

BIA   Brick Institute of America
            (Formerly SCPI)
            1750 Old Meadow Road; McLean VA 22101; 703/893-4010,

BSI   Building Stone Institute
            420 Lexington Avenue; New York NY 10017; 202/532-9477

CDA   Copper Development Association, Inc.
            405 Lexington Avenue; New York, NY 10017; 202/953-7300

CRA   California Redwood Association
            617 Montgomery; San Francisco, CA 94111; 415/392-7880

CRI   The Carpet and Rug Institute
            P.O. Box 2048; Dalton, GA 30720; 404/278-3176

CRSI   Concrete Reinforcing Steel Institute
            180 North LaSalle Street; Chicago, IL 60601; 312/372-5059

CS   Commercial Standard of the NBS
            (U.S. Department of Commerce)
            Government Printing Office; Washington, DC 20402

CSI	The Construction Specifications Institute, Inc. 1150 17th Street, NW; Washington, DC 20036; 202/833-2160
DHI	Door & Hardware Institute 1815 North Fort Myer; Arlington, VA 22209; 703/527-2060
FM	Factory Mutual Engineering Corp. 1151 Boston-Providence Turnpike; Norwood, MA 02062; 617/762-4300
FPL	Forest Products Laboratory (U.S. Department of Agriculture) North Walnut Street; Madison, WI 53705
FS	Federal Specification (General Services Administration) Building 197, Washington Navy Yard SE; Washington, DC 20407
FTI	Facing Tile Institute 500 12th Street, SW; Washington, DC 20024; 202/484-5558
GA	Gypsum Association 1603 Orrington Avenue; Evanston, IL 60201; 312/491-1744
GSA	General Services Administration 19th & F Streets, NW; Washington, DC 20405
GTA	Glass Tempering Association 3310 Harrison; Topeka, KS 66611; 913/266-7064
HPMA	Hardwood Plywood Manufacturers Association P.O. Box 6246; Arlington, VA 22206; 703/671-6262
ILI	Indiana Limestone Institute of America, Inc. Stone City Bank Building; Bedford, IN 47421; 812/275-4426
IMI	International Masonry Institute 823 15th Street, NW; Washington, DC 20005; 202/783-3908
IRA	Industrial Risk Insurers (Formerly FIA) 85 Woodland Street; Hartford, CT 06102; 203/525-2601
LIA	Lead Industries Association 292 Madison Avenue; New York, NY 10017; 202/783-3908
MBMA	Metal Building Manufacturers' Association 2130 Keith Building; Cleveland, OH 44115; 216/241-7333
MFMA	Maple Flooring Manufacturers Association 424 Washington Avenue; Oshkosh, WI 54901; 414/233-1920
MIA	Marble Institute of America 60 Plato Avenue; St. Paul, MN 55107; 612/222-4759
MIL	Military Standardization Documents (U.S. Department of Defense) Naval Publications and Forms Center 5801 Tabor Avenue; Philadelphia, PA 19120
MLSFA	Metal Lath/Steel Framing Association 221 North LaSalle Street; Chicago, IL 60601; 312/346-1862
NAAMM	The National Association of Architectural Metal Manufacturers 1033 South Boulevard; Oak Park, IL 60302; 312/383-7725

NAPF   National Association of Plastic Fabricators, Inc.
                4720 Montgomery Lane; Bethesda, MD 20014; 202/656-8874

NAV-FAC   Naval Facilities Engineering Command (Guide Specs)
                (U.S. Department of the Navy)
                200 Stovall Street; Alexandria, VA 22332

NBFU   National Board of Fire Underwriters
                (See listing under A.I.A.)

NBGQA   National Building Granite Quarries Association, Inc.
                P.O. Box 444; Concord, NH 03302

NBHA   National Builders' Hardware Association
                (See listing under DHI)

NBS   National Bureau of Standards
                (U.S. Department of Commerce)
                Gaithersburg, MD 20234

NCMA   National Concrete Masonry Association
                6845 Elm Street; McLean, VA 22101; 703/790-8650

NEC   National Electrical Code (by NFPA)

NEI   National Elevator Industry, Inc.
                600 Third Avenue; New York, NY 10016; 212/986-1545

NEMA   National Electrical Manufacturers Association
                155 East 44th Street; New York, NY 10017; 212/682-1500

NFPA   National Fire Protection Association
                470 Atlantic Avenue; Boston, MA 02210; 617/482-8755

N.F.P.A.   National Forest Products Association
                (Successor to NLMA)
                1619 Massachusetts Avenue, NW; Washington, DC 20036;
                    202/332-1050

NHLA   National Hardwood Lumber Association
                332 South Michigan Avenue; Chicago, IL 60604; 312/427-2810

NKCA   National Kitchen Cabinet Association
                334 East Broadway; Louisville, KY 40202; 502/582-2619

NOFMA   National Oak Flooring Manufacturers Association
                814 Sterick Building; Memphis, TN 38103; 901/526-5016

NPA   National Particleboard Association
                2306 Perkins Place; Silver Spring, MD 20910; 301/587-2204

NPCA   National Paint and Coatings Association
                (Formerly NPVLMA)
                1500 Rhode Island, NW; Washington, DC 20005; 202/462-6272

NRMCA   National Ready Mixed Concrete Association
                900 Spring Street; Silver Spring, MD 20910; 301/587-1400

NSF   National Sanitation Foundation
                3475 Plymouth Road; Ann Arbor, MI 48106; 313/769-8010

NSPE   National Society of Professional Engineers
                2029 K Street, NW; Washington, DC 20006; 202/331-7020

NSSEA   National School Supply & Equipment Association
                1500 Wilson Boulevard; Arlington, VA 22209; 703/524-8819

NTMA   The National Terrazzo and Mosaic Association, Inc.
2-A West Loudoun Street; Leesburg, VA 22075; 703/777-7683

NWMA   National Woodwork Manufacturers Association, Inc.
400 West Madison Street; Chicago, IL 60606; 312/782-6232

OSHA   Occupational Safety & Health Administration
(U.S. Department of Labor)
Government Printing Office; Washington, DC 20402

PBS   Public Building Services of GSA
19th & F Streets, NW; Washington, DC 20405

PCA   Portland Cement Association
5420 Old Orchard Road; Skokie, IL 60076; 312/966-6200

PCI   Prestressed Concrete Institute
20 North Wacker Drive; Chicago, IL 60606; 312/346-4071

PEI   Porcelain Enamel Institute, Inc.
1911 North Fort Myer; Arlington, VA 22209; 703/527-5257

PLIB   Pacific Lumber Inspection Bureau
White-Henry-Stuart Building; Seattle, WA 98101

PS   Product Standard of NBS
(U.S. Department of Commerce)
Government Printing Office; Washington, DC 20402

RCRBSJ   Research Council on Riveted & Bolted Structural Joints
1717 East Ninth Street; Cleveland, OH 44113; 216/241-1482

RFCI   Resilient Floor Covering Institute
26 Washington Street; East Orange, NJ 07017; 201/674-3225

RIS   Redwood Inspection Service (Grading Rules)
627 Montgomery; San Francisco, CA 94111;

RTI   Resilient Tile Institute
(See listing under RFCI)

SAMA   Scientific Apparatus Makers Association
1140 Connecticut, NW; Washington, DC 20036; 202/223-1360

SDI   Steel Deck Institute
P.O. Box 3812; St. Louis, MO 63122; 314/965-1741

S.D.I.   Steel Door Institute
2130 Keith Building; Cleveland, OH 44115; 216/241-7333

SFPA   Southern Forest Products Association
(Formerly Southern Pine Association)
P.O. Box 52468; New Orleans, LA 70152; 504/834-8544

SHLMA   Southern Hardwood Lumber Manufacturers Association
805 Sterick Building; Memphis, TN 38103; 901/525-8221

SIGMA   Sealed Insulating Glass Manufacturers Association
1629 K Street, NW; Washington, DC 20006; 202/466-8693

SJI   Steel Joist Institute
2001 Jefferson Davis Highway; Arlington, VA 22202; 703/920-1700

SMACNA   Sheet Metal & Air Conditioning Contractors National Association, Inc.
8224 Old Courthouse Road; Tysons Corner, Vienna, VA 22180;
703/790-7980

SPI	The Society of the Plastics Industry, Inc.
	355 Lexington Avenue; New York, NY 10017; 212/573-9400
SPIB	Southern Pine Inspection Bureau (Grading Rules)
	P.O. Box 846; Pensacola, FL 32594; 904/434-2611
SPR	Simplified Practice Recommendation of NBS
	(U.S. Department of Commerce)
	Government Printing Office; Washington, DC 20402
SSPC	Steel Structures Painting Council
	4400 Fifth Avenue; Pittsburgh, PA 15213; 412/621-1100
SWI	Steel Window Institute
	2130 Keith Building; Cleveland, OH 44115; 216-241-7333
TCA	Tile Council of America, Inc.
	P.O. Box 326; Princeton, NJ 08540; 609/921-7050
UL	Underwriters Laboratories, Inc.
	207 East Ohio Street; Chicago, IL 60611; 312/642-6969
WCLA	West Coast Lumbermen's Association
	(See listing under WWPA)
WCLB	West Coast Lumber Inspection Bureau (Grading Rules)
	P.O. Box 23145; Portland, OR 97223; 503/639-0651
WIC	Woodwork Institute of California
	P.O. Box 1666; Fresno, CA 93717
WMA	Wallcovering Manufacturers Association
	1099 Wall Street West; Lyndhurst, NJ 07071; 201/935-2577
WRI	Wire Reinforcement Institute
	7900 Westpark Drive; McLean, VA 22101; 703/790-9790
WSFI	Wood & Synthetic Flooring Institute
	1201 Waukegan Road; Glenview, IL 60025; 312/724-7700
WWPA	Western Wood Products Association (Grading Rules)
	1500 Yeon Building; Portland, OR 97204; 503/224-3930
WWPA	Woven Wire Products Association
	108 West Lake Street; Chicago, IL 60601; 312/332-6502

Index

Accounting Department, 1
Acoustical Ceilings, Hung, 127, 128, 132
  Concealed Spline, 127
  Exposed T, 127
  Suspension Systems, 128
Adjacent Structures, 20
  Information Required, 20, 21
  Owner, 20
  Stability, 20
Air Conditioning, 12, 145
  Balancing, 146
  Controls, 146
  Duct Work, 145
  Equipment Supports, 111, 112
  Field Measurements, 145
  Field Sketches, 145
  Insulation, 146
  Systems, 146
Anchor Bolts, 108, 111, 112, 138, 142
Architect, 15, 80, 105, 131, 150
Assistant Superintendent, 13
  Responsibilities, 13

Backfilling, 100
Base Plates, 108
  Grouting, 108
Batter Boards, 22, 23
Bench Mark, 10, 11
Boilers, 145
Boring Logs, 28
Brick, 104
  Seat, 100
Building Code, 21, 26

Caissons, 26
Carpenter, 104, 116, 141

Carpentry, 114
Carpeting, 128
  Floor Preparation, 128
Casework, 135
Cast Iron Frame, 108, 111, 112
Catalog Cuts, 133
Ceiling Lights, 66
Ceramic Tile, 130
  Adhesive, 130
  Floors, 130
  Thin-Set, 130
  Walls, 130
Chainmen, 9
Chalk Boards, 133
Changes, 15
Change Orders, 15
Check List
  Carpentry and Millwork, 117
  Concrete, 99
  Conveying Equipment, 143
  Electrical, 149
  Excavation, Pile Foundations and Dewatering, 28
  Finishing Trades, 132
  Furnishing, 138, 139
  General Conditions, 19
  Hollow Metal, Hardware, Entrances, Windows, 124
  Masonry, 106, 107
  Mechanical Trades, 147
  Miscellaneous Specialties, 136
  Roofing, Sheetmetal, Waterproofing, 121
  Special Construction, 141
  Structural Steel and Miscellaneous Metal, 113
Clean Up, 104, 150, 151

Coffer Dams, 26
Cold Rooms, 140
  Aggregates, 31, 32
    Course, 28
    Crushed Stone, 61, 65
    Gravel, 6, 61
    Segregation, 78
  Air Entrained, 29
  Anchors, 66
    Brick, 66
    Slots, 66
  Buggies, Concrete, 38, 44, 74, 77
  Cement Mason, 78
  Chamfer Strips, 38
  Chutes, Types, 39, 44
  Clamps, 47
    Column, 36, 37, 66
  Cold Joints, 78
  Column Fireproofing, 38
  Concrete Bucket, 73
  Concrete Run Panels, 73, 74
  Construction Joints, 85
  Crane, 54, 66
    Chicago Boom, 75
    Climbing, 77
    Truck, 77
  Curing, 44
  Design and Tests, 29
    Air Entrained, 29
    Design Mix, 29
    Field Sampling, 29
    Slump, 29
    Strength, 30
    Test Cylinders, 29
    Testing Lab, 29
  Engineer, 79
    Job, 79
    Structural, 79, 80
  Flat Slab Floors, 65, 66
    Drop Panel, 66
  Floor Hardeners, 98, 99
  Form
    Coatings, 91
    Ties, 46
    Yard, 54
  Forms
    Columns, 37, 46, 47, 54
    Floor, 61, 66
    Metal, 47, 54, 66
    Spandrel Beams, 66

    Stringers, 66
    Wall, 44, 45, 78
  Fundamental Facts, 29, 30
  Hoist Tower, 44, 75
  Honeycomb, 38, 44, 78
  Hopper, 78
  Job Staff, 79, 80
  Keyway, 38, 78
  Lime and Grade, 66
  Lumber, Dressed, 54
  Moist Curing, 30
  Mortar, 38
  Moving Concrete, 38
  Mud Sills, 61, 66
  Plywood, 44, 45, 46, 54, 66
  Polyethylene Film, Use, 87
  Portland Cement, Types, 30, 31
  Pouring Concrete, 32
    Basement Walls, 78
    Columns, 47
    Floor Slabs, 44, 73
    Footings, 32, 33
    General, 32
    Grade Beams, 32
    Metal Deck, 92
    Monolithic, 47
    Pile Caps, 32, 33
    Reinforced Concrete Building, 33, 36, 37, 38
    Structural Steel Buildings, 33, 36, 37, 38
  Radiant Heating, 97, 98
  Receiving Hoppers, 39, 44
  Reinforcing Steel, 39
    Accessories, 66, 85
    Bar Sizes, 80
    Basic Design, 79
    Beam Bolstars, 75
    Bending on Job, 82
    Bending Schedule, 79
    Chairs, 79
    Classification, 82
    Clearances, 79
    Mill Cut and Bent, 82
    Placement, 80, 82, 83, 84, 85, 87
    Reinforcing Rods, 61, 68
    Spacing, 79
    Splices, 79
    Storage, 80, 81
    Supply and Delivery, 80, 85

Resistance to Freezing and Thawing, 30
Rubbing, 38
Sand, 28
Sand Grout, 44, 47
Scaffold, 78
  Rolling, 78
  Square, 65, 66
Segregation, 38, 44
Shores, 54, 65, 66, 67
  Adjustable Patented, 65
  Re shores, 61, 77
Sleeves, 66
Spreaders, 65, 66
  Floor, 65
Stirrups, 79
Stripping, 46, 66
  Floor Forms, 77
  Hook, 78
Studs, 46
Vibrators, 28, 85
Walers, 45, 46, 54
Wall Ties, 46
Wedges, 47
  Cast Metal, 46, 47
Winter Weather Operation, 42, 93, 94,
  95
  Canvas, 92, 93, 94, 95
  Fire Protection, 95
  Heatable Storage Tank, 94
  Salamanders, 92, 93, 94, 96
  Salt Hay, 92, 93, 95
  Space Heaters, 92, 93
  Temperature Records, 95
  Watchmen, 93, 96
  Wire Rope Cable Sling, 75
  Wood Cleats, 54, 65
  Wood Horses, 73, 75
Concrete Superintendent, 11
Conductive Floor, 130
Conduits, 125
Containers, 151
Contract, 2
  Items, 8
Coordinate Lines, 11
Coordination Drawings, 11
Coordination of Trades, 12, 151
  Concrete, 133, 138, 144, 145, 148
  Electrical, 104, 134, 135, 146, 148, 149
  Finishing, 146, 148
  Masonry, 148

  Mechanical, 104, 136, 144
  Plumbing, 136, 144, 145
  Roofing, 145
  Steel, 145, 148
Coping, 105
Cost, 150
  Engineer, 12
  Overruns, 150
  Studies, 12
Cost Plus Job, 12
CPM, 2, 7
Curbs, Pre-Fabricated, 145
Curtain Wall Construction, 123

Dam Construction, 2
Damproofing, 100, 119, 120
Dealers, Material, Equipment, 15, 16
Decisions, 9
Defusers, 128
Dewatering, 26, 27
Directories, 133
Documents Required, 2
Doors and Frames, 123, 131
  Aluminum, 123
  Borrowed Lights, 124
  Stainless Steel, 123
  Steel, *see* Hollow Metal (H.M.)
Drywall Construction, 126
  Joint Patching, 131
  Sanding, 131
  Sheetrock, 126, 131, 141
  Taping Application, 126
  Taping Compound, 126
Dumbwaiters, 142

Electrical, 148, 149
  Control Wiring, 148
  Coordination, 148, 149
    Ceilings, 148
    HVAC Systems and Equipment, 148,
    149
  Emergency Generator, 148
  Foreman, 149
  Lighting, 148
  Motor Control Panel, 148
  Power, 148
  Service, 6, 142, 148
  Switch Gear, 148
  Temporary Light and Power, 148
  Wiring Diagrams, 149

Elevator, 142
  Building, 101
Employer, 151
Engineer, 79, 140, 150
Equipment, 11
  Approval, 145
  Attachments, 125, 136
  Bases, Concrete, 133
  Details, 135
  Detention, 135, 136
  Food Service, 135, 136
  Library, 135, 136
  Loading Dock, 135, 136
  Solar Energy, 140
  Steam Bath, 140
  Storage, 136
Estimating Department, 13
Estimator, 1, 2
Excavation, 20, 22
  Access for Concrete Pour, 23
  Classification, 24
  Contractor, 21
  Fill, 22
  Footings, 22, 23
  Payment, Unit Price, 24
  Ramps, Earth, Timber, 23
  Sheeted, 27
  Shoring, 24
  Water in, 22
Expansion Bolts, 108
Expansion Joints, 119
Expediter, 15
Expediting, 15

Field, 1, 2, 3
  Changes, 146
  Force, 1, 2, 13
  Measurements, 117
  Preparation, 113
Finish Schedule, Room, 18
Finishing Trades, 132, 146
Fireproof Buildings, 115
Flag Poles, 133
Flashing, 100, 118
  Cap, 118
  Drains, 118
  Material, 118
  Spandrel, 100, 118
  Through-Wall, 118
Flooring Systems, 130, 133

Access Floors, 133
  Computer Floors, 133
  Miscellaneous, 130
Furnishings, 138
  Attachments, 138
  Draperies, 138
  Mats, 138
  Seating, Public, 138
  Shades, 138
  Supports, Built in, 138
  Venetian Blinds, 138

General Contractor, 5
  Foreman, 5
  Own Forces, 3, 4
Glass and Glazing, 123, 124

H.V.A.C. Contractor, 12, 112, 145
  Heating System, 146
  Temporary Heat, 146
Hardware, 116, 122, 131
  Butts, 116
  Closures, 116, 123
  Cutouts, 116
  Delivery Time, 122
  Expediting, 122
  Face Plates, 116
  Item Numbers Marking, 122
  Kick Plates, 116
  Locks, 116
  Panic Bolts, 116
  Schedule, 122
  Storage, 122
  Supplier, 122
Hoists, 100
  Fixed, 100
  Rubber Tire, 100
  Tower, 100
Hollow Metal (H.M.), 115, 116, 122
  Door Bucks, 14, 102, 115, 119, 122, 131,
    141
  Doors, 115, 116, 122, 141
  Installation, 115, 116
  Knock Down Bucks, 116
  Spreader Sticks, 116
  Sub Bucks, 116
  Tagging, 122
  Trimmed Openings, 116
  Welded Frames, 116
Home Office, 15, 19, 131

Notification, 15

Industrial Standards, 153, 154, 155, 156, 157, 158
Inserts, 102, 123, 145
Inspector, 15
Instrument Man, 9
Insulation, 119
  Cavity Wall, 119
  Interior, Walls and Ceilings, 119
  Perimeter, 119
  Roofing, 119
Integrated Drawings, 11, 12, 144, 145

Job
  Delays, 15
  Engineer, 13
  Items, 7
  Meetings, 13, 16, 152
  Reports, 8
  Running, The, 19
  Staff, 4, 6, 151
    Harmony, 15
    Organization, 4, 6

Labor Commitments, 2
Laminated Beams and Girders, 116
Lathing, 125, 127
  Corner Beads, 125
  Expansion Beads, 125
  Furring, 125, 127
  Installation, 125, 127
  Material, 125
  Stop Beads, 127
  Studding, 125
Lead-lined walls, 141
Leveling Plates, 108
Lighting, 127, 131
  Fixtures, 127
Line and Grade, 9, 10
Lintel, 100, 105
  Line, 17
  Loose, 11, 109, 112
  Setting, 109
Load Test, 25
Lockers, 133
Louvres, 102, 133
Lumber, 115
  Fire Retardent, 115
  Plastic Laminate, 111

Wolminized Treated, 115

Main Office, 15
Masonry, 15
  Access, 102
  Built-in Items, 102
  Cleaning, 104
  Contractor, 100, 109
  Coursing, 100, 109
  Exterior Walls, 100
  Foreman, 100
  Plant, 100
  Preparation, 100
  Reinforcement, 101
  Rubble, 104
  Storage, 104
  Superintendent, 100
  Walls, 115, 120, 131, 141
  Walls, Type, 101, 102
Masonry Accessories, 101
  Brick Ties, 101
  Drip Ties, 102
  Inserts, 102
  Specials, 101
  Weep Holes, 101
Material
  Conveyors, 142
  Estimated, 13
  Lifts, 142
  Masonry, 106, 107
  Quantities, 13
Mechanical, 145
  Contractor, 145, 148
  Drawings, Equipment, 145
  Drawings Sleeve Location, 145
  Engineer, 15
  Trade Classifications, 146, 147
  Trades, 35, 66, 136, 144
Millwork, 114, 116
  Counters, 114
  Delivery, 114, 116
  Plastic Laminate, 111
Miscellaneous Metal, 108
  Items, 109, 111
Miscellaneous Specialties, 133
Moisture Meter, 131
Mortar, 102, 106
  Nonstaining, 106
  Test, 102
Moving Stairs and Walks, 142

Multistory Buildings, 144, 148

New Materials and Methods, 16

Office, 3
  Personnel, 146
Office Force, 1
OSHA, 18
Owner, 2, 150
  Representative, 151
Owner's Representative, 15, 16

Painting, 113
  Paint Colors, 131
  Paint Manufacturer's Literature, 131
  Prime Coat, 131
  Unpainted Surfaces, 131
Partitions, 104, 127, 133
  Coiling, 133
  Folding, 133
  Interior, 104
  Movable, 127
  Sliding, 133
  Toilet, 133
Party Chief, 9, 10
Pay Phone, 19
Payroll, 19
  Department, 19
Penetration Drawings, 135
Permits, 2, 108, 147
Pert, 2
Piles, 24, 25
  Class, 24, 25
  Type, 24, 25, 26
Pile Driving, Equipment, 25
Pile Foundation, 24, 25
Pipes, 108, 125
  Chases, 144
  Concealed, 145
  Piping, 1
  Supports, 108
Plans and Specifications, 3
Plant Layout, 3
Plaster, 14, 114, 125, 127
  Application, 146
  Ceilings, Hung, 127
  Grounds, 126
  Rings, 127
  Types, 125
  Walls, 131

Plumbing, 144
  Clean Outs, 144
  Contractor, 12, 136, 144
  Drawings, 145
  Scheduling, 145
  Slab Pour, 145
  Temporary Water, 147
  Tests, 145
  Trade, 146, 147
Productivity, Control, 12
Progress of Job, 8
Progress Schedule, 2, 7, 8
  Bar Chart, 7
  CPM, 7
  Pert, 2
Project Manager, 1, 12
Punch List, 131, 151
Purchasing, 1
  Agent, 1
  Department, 80

Quarry Tile, 130
  Bases, 136
  Floors, 130

Radiation Protection
  Material, 140, 141
  Records, 151
Reinforced Concrete Building, 10, 33, 36,
  37, 38
Resilient Floor, 128, 132
  Preparation, 128
  Vinyl Asbestos Tile (Vat), 128
Road Building, 2
Roads, 21
  Permanent, 21
  Site, 21
Roofing, 118
  Pitch Pockets, 118
  Sheet Metal, 118
  Surface Preparation, 118

Safety, 16
  Protection of the Public, 109
  Requirements, 109, 124
Saunas, 140
Scaffolding, 100, 104
  Exterior, 100
  Hanging, 100
  Pipe, 100

Wood, 100
Sealants, 119
  Where used, 119
Service Walkways, 111
Sewer System, 2
Shanties, 5
  Job Office, 5, 6
  Workmen's Facilities, 6
Shop Drawings, 3, 11, 112, 117, 123, 133,
    136, 140, 142, 145
Sidewalk Bridge, 109
Signs, 133
Sills, 105
Sire, Access, 21
Snot Stick, 102
Spandrel Beams, 11, 102
Specification, 2, 26, 106
Spray Fireproofing, 126
  Installation, 126
Sprinkler, 146
  Alarm Controls, 146
  Dry System, 146
  Wet System, 146
Steel
  Deck, 108, 126
  Erection, 108
  Erectors, 11, 108
  Framed Buildings, 11
  Framing, 133
  Joists, 108
  Sleeves, 112, 135, 144
  Stairs, 109, 111
  Storage, 108
  Structural, 108, 126
  Supports, 133
Stone, 105
  Cast, 105
  Coping, 118
  Erection, 105, 106
  Granite, 105, 106
  Limestone, 105, 106
  Marble, 105
  Masonry Backup, 106
  Natural, 105
  Sandstone, 105
Storage of Material, 3, 136
Stone Fronts, 123
Structural Engineer, 25, 79
Subcontractor, 15, 150, 151
  Contractural Share, 150

Required, 6
  Work Force, 150
Superintendent, 14
  Walk the Job, 14
  Work Assignments, 14
Surface Runoff, 27
Surveyor, 10, 108
  Building Line Limits, 100
  Grade Crew, 10
  Licensed, 10
  Line and Grade, 100
  Wall Limes, 145
Swimming Pools, 140

Telephone Enclosures, 133
Templates, 102
Temporary Services, 132, 146, 147, 148,
    149
  Electrical Contractor, 148, 149
  Equipment, 132
  HVAC Contractor, 146
  Light and Power, 148
  Water, 147
Terrazzo, 125
  Bases, 136
  Contractor, 129
  Dividing Strips, 128
  Types, 129
Time Extensions, 15
Tiolet Accessories, 133
  Accessories, 133
  Chemical, 6
  Facilities, 6

Underpinning Contractor, 21
Unit Cost, 13

Vinyl Wall Covering, 131

Wallpaper, 131
Wardrobes, 133
Water, 2, 28
  System, 2
  Table, 28
  Works, 2
Waterproofing, 119
  Cement, 119
  Ionite, 119
Wellpoint System, 27
Wet Trades, 14

Windows, 102, 114, 123, 119
Winter Heat, 150
  Winter Weather Operation, *see* Cold
    Rooms, Winter Weather Operation
Wood
  Blocking, 114, 133,
    138
  Doors, 116
  Framing, 114, 116
  Grounds, 114, 117, 136

  Panelling, 114
  Shelving, 114
  Sleepers, 129
  Studding, 141
  Windows, 102, 114
Wood Floors, 129
  Installation, 129, 130
  Parquet, 130
  Sleepers, 129
Written Confirmation, 8